TACTICAL ECONOMICS

TACTICAL ECONOMICS

Investment Strategy in a Changing Economy

Daniel A. Blumberg

Consolidated
Capital
Communications
Group, Inc.

DEDICATION
To Adrian, a very special lady

Jacket and Book Design by Fifth Street Design, Berkeley, CA.

Printed in the United States of America

Portions of this book were originally published in *Pension World, Tax Shelter Digest, The Financial Planner, Mortgage Banking, Registered Representative, National Underwriter, Real Estate Review, AAII Journal, Financial Planning Today,* and *Research.*

Library of Congress Cataloging in Publication Data

Blumberg, Daniel A., 1938–
   Tactical Economics.

   Includes index.
   1. Investments — United States — Handbooks, manuals, etc.
I. Title.
HG4921.B58   1984   332.6'78   83-26141
ISBN 0-930032-05-5

Table of Contents

A simple method for calculating risk and reward for *any* potential investment.

Risk and risk-mitigating factors.

Figures

Foreword

I've often been asked, "Where do top pros like yourself turn when you're looking for investment advice?" One answer that comes immediately to mind is Dan Blumberg. Whenever I see an article by Dan, I turn right to it because I know it will offer new insights and information that will help me make investment decisions. Dan's writing offers a rare combination: broad perspective with an eagle eye for detail. The bottom line for him is always to determine reasonable and logical methods for evaluating investments.

I'm delighted to see this volume in which Dan addresses a variety of investment opportunities. The full breadth of Dan Blumberg's perception can now be appreciated. Whether your interest is the stock market, gold, or real estate, whether you want to learn about supply-side economics, debt financing, or investment relativity, Dan Blumberg has a unique ability to capture the large picture — and explain complex issues in a clear, pragmatic way. This book is must reading for every investment professional who likes to make his or her own decisions.

Venita VanCaspel

Preface

There are two kinds of economists — theoretical economists and tactical economists.

Theoretical economists most often have advanced academic degrees; they advise presidents and write learned articles. Tactical economists have a very limited and specific interest in economics — they are concerned with how economic conditions will affect their own or their clients' net worth. Tactical economists include the auto mechanic who starts stockpiling used Mercedes parts because he *knows* all those seven- to ten-year-old Mercedes he sees on the streets are going to need repairs in the next few years. Another tactical economist is the gold bullion trader who buys during a momentary improvement of cold war tensions (e.g., the signing of an international accord) because she *knows* that the next disruptive political event will cause the price of gold to dramatically increase.

The differences in orientation between theoretical economists and tactical economists are readily apparent. The former study economics as a science for its own sake, and they are fascinated by the process of developing new causal explanations for economic phenomena. The latter are far less interested in such theories than in the *results* of economic changes, and how those results affect their personal economic goals. A second crucial difference is that theoretical economists do not venture capital, thus their prognostications are basically risk-free. Tactical economists have no such margin: if they are wrong, they lose money.

Tactical economics is thus the economics of strategy. Given certain economic phenomena, such as ballooning budget deficits, or an oil glut, or the devaluation of a currency, tactical economists first try to predict these events' effect on a wide variety of investment vehicles: gold, real estate, stocks, bonds, or oil, for instance. Their next concern is to reposition assets in such a way that they minimize their financial risks and maximize their economic advantages.

How do you identify a tactical economist? By the success of his or her tactics. The tactical economist is by definition someone who devises investment strategies, someone whose record of investment successes testifies to a thorough understanding of the realities of the marketplace.

By all measures, Daniel Blumberg is a tactical economist *par excellence*. A successful financier, co-founder and a dynamic leader of the nation's largest sponsor of public real estate investment programs, he is a twenty-year veteran of the front-line trenches of investing. He has established an unparalleled record of tactical success that has greatly benefited thousands of investors who have relied on his analyses.

What makes Dan Blumberg truly unique, however, is his ability as a writer. He has a rare talent for making the complex easy to understand, for pointing directly to the key issues, and for offering straightforward guidelines and alternatives — all of which help his readers to make their own investment decisions.

Most of the chapters in this book have their origins in articles written for *Mortgage Banking, The Financial Planner, Pension World, Registered Representative, Pension and Investment Age, Tax Shelter Digest, National Underwriter, Real Estate Review,* and *Financial Planning Today* — all publications for financial professionals. Selected from the author's numerous contributions to these professional journals, this set of articles is of broad interest to professionals and investors alike throughout the investment community. Each chapter records the reactions of a savvy investment professional — responsible for millions, and more recently, billions of dollars of invested capital — to the vagaries of the economy and the financial marketplace.

Tom Elliott
Editor, *Research*

Acknowledgements

The fact that this book is a reality is a tribute to the patience, editorial skills, and enthusiasm of the talented people with whom I collaborated. I am pleased to acknowledge the dedication and assistance given this project by my secretary and friend, Jean Finkbeiner, always encouraging and organized. My thanks also go to: Betty Matthias, long-time friend and business associate, whose editorial skills were invaluable; Richard Wollack, my business partner and publisher; Jim Miller, chief editor; Amy Einsohn, Didi Goodman and Roger Rapoport, who did the final editing; and last, but not least, all of my business colleagues at the Consolidated Capital companies who offered me the encouragement and freedom of time to write. To all of these good people with whom I shared the work that went into the book, I also share the credit for whatever success it may enjoy.

Introduction

This book is addressed to readers who have enough income to meet their current expenses and now want to concentrate on obtaining financial independence. In my twenty years of experience as an investment advisor, I've helped many clients substantially increase their net worth — and this book can help you do the same for yourself.

In order to become a successful investor, you must first appreciate one simple principle: *In today's economy, yesterday's rules don't necessarily apply*. Above all else, successful investment strategy depends on a broad knowledge of the current economic environment and a careful comparison of available investment opportunities.

Thus the savvy investor will first want to understand those current regional, national, and international economic conditions that influence investment results. Acquiring such broad and timely knowledge of local, national, and global economic environments, markets, and values is difficult for most of us, however, because we don't have the time to gather all the information and we lack the training to interpret and integrate all the bits of data. Most investors tend, therefore, to make investment decisions much in the same way that they make other decisions — based on experience. But in today's rapidly changing economic environment, their experience may no longer be relevant.

Furthermore, I'm thoroughly convinced that no one should base investment decisions on how he or she thinks events might, could, or should turn out. It is far more prudent to risk one's capital on an understanding of *what is* rather than on hunches about *what might be*. True, a big profit is often the reward for accurate guesses about how things might go — but the penalty or loss for incorrect guesses can also be sizable.

So, to help you make better-informed investment decisions, I devote the first part of this book to a survey of selected economic conditions and trends, and how these relate to investment strategy in the mid 1980s. Among the topics covered are: inflation, interest rates, the federal deficit and money supply, productivity, foreign exchange rates, market supply and demand, and government regulation.

Armed with an understanding of actual economic conditions, an investor is ready to evaluate a variety of investment opportunities. Many investors will begin by simply asking themselves, Is this a good investment? That's a reasonable question, but *not* the most important one. Instead, the smart investor will ask, Is this the best investment opportunity for me, given *my current goals* and the *alternatives available to me*? Although no amount of analysis can remove all the risk from an investment decision, by comparing the risks and rewards of various opportunities, investors can increase their chances for success.

In the second part of this book I turn to the specific evaluation of an alternative that I think represents a source of very profitable investments in 1984 and 1985: real estate and, in particular, real estate investment partnerships. In these chapters I compare real estate with several other types of investments and discuss relevant tax planning considerations. More specific techniques for evaluating potential real estate investments and increasing profits are presented in the third part of the book, with a consideration of creative financing, internal rate of return, and similar topics.

IDEAL INVESTMENT PORTFOLIO FOR 1984–1985 My recommendation for the ideal portfolio for 1984– 1985 is based on two assumptions. First, recent volatility in the inflation and growth rates suggests that *diversification* is the best single rule for developing an investment portfolio. Second, I believe that the current low rate of inflation and relatively high growth will continue through the first quarter of 1985. Consider the following factors: we still have high unemployment and a relatively tight money policy; unused industrial capacity is high, manufacturers' inventories are low, and unfilled orders for producer goods are relatively high. In sum, the prospects for economic growth are strong, while the forces that cause runaway inflation are largely absent.

Given these two assumptions, my suggestion for the ideal investment portfolio is: 40 percent real estate (housing or commercial), 40 percent stocks, 15 percent money market instruments, and 5 percent hard currency in the form of gold, silver, or platinum. I would keep 15 percent in money market instruments to take advantage of opportunities as they arise or emergencies that require ready cash. (I sleep better knowing I won't have to sell property or stock in a hurry to raise cash.) And the reason I do not have larger investments in stocks is that I prefer to have a sizable part of my portfolio in real estate at today's prices, which I consider to be bargains compared to the prices I expect thirty-six months from now. It's important to note that an investor should not consider his or her home as part of the investment portfolio when determining the proper portfolio mix.

Let me conclude these introductory remarks by briefly addressing the issue that most perplexes investors at this time: fear of higher interest rates. The main reason that rates are high now is that both the private sector and the public sector are competing for capital in the marketplace at the same time that the Federal Reserve is pursuing a tight money policy. These conditions keep interest rates high, but neither the Federal Reserve, nor the Reagan administration, nor the Congress wants to see interest rates so high as to abort the recovery. Thus should the prime rate reach 13 percent, I think that the Federal Reserve would commit

ARE HIGHER INTEREST RATES AHEAD?

itself to at least three of the following four activities: pump reserves into the system through open market operation, drop the discount rate, reduce bank reserve requirements, and fund part of the federal deficit by printing money.

These activities should guarantee a lower interest rate in the short run (six to twelve months). Ultimately, of course, the cost of money will always be determined by supply and demand, but in the short term lower interest rates can be manipulated, and the pressures on the Fed to do so will come from no less than President Reagan, his closest economic advisors, and a host of Congressional members seeking re-election in November 1984.

Thus economic and political considerations lead me to expect real economic growth between 4 and 5 percent, inflation at 3.5 to 4.5 percent, and a prime rate no higher than 10 percent by the start of the second quarter of 1984.

December 30, 1983

Part
One

Economics
for Investors

*Chapter
One*

*The National
Economy in 1984:
Analysis and
Forecast*

To the delight of many, key indicators are pointing toward a solid recovery for the American economy. Today the question for the seasoned investor is not how to protect oneself against recession but how to take advantage of the current recovery. Right now tactical investors are repositioning their assets to take advantage of good times. They expect the economy to brighten in the months ahead for several reasons. Among them are half a dozen factors contributing to increased productivity and a higher gross national product.

- On the regulatory and government side they include an increasing money supply and the Reagan administration's $35 billion tax cut that took effect in July 1983.
- In the business sector we have 29 percent un-used industrial capacity and a booming stock market.
- On the consumer side there is pent-up demand, buyer optimism, and a higher rate of personal savings.

By themselves these factors might not add up to such a positive short term picture. But when you add in a structural inflation rate of 3 to 4 percent, the lowest since the 1950's, prospects brighten considerably. As long as a large part of productivity increases continue coming from previously idle industrial plants, the demand for new capital will remain moderate, and the inflation rate should be relatively stable. Barring a catastrophe such as war in the Middle East or very poor agricultural production, chances of renewed high inflation appear slim.

Even a $200 billion federal budget deficit need not squelch the recovery — if the money supply expands enough to meet the Treasury's needs and continue serving the private sector. This was the case during the first five months of 1983: interest rates fell despite unprecedented borrowing by the Treasury. And the booming economy has also eased the credit crunch in the private sector. Buoyed by surging deposits, financial institutions suddenly find their loan funds exceed the supply of credit-worthy borrowers. The federal funds rate (the rate banks charge each other for overnight money) has been dropping for the same reason.

INCREASING MONEY SUPPLY

The money supply, as measured by M-1 (currency and demand checking accounts) and M-2 (currency and demand checking accounts plus savings and money market demand accounts), has been rising at historically high rates (see Figure 1). For example, in March 1983, M-2 was growing at an annually compounded rate of 27 percent and M-1 at a rate of 10 percent — rates substantially higher than the Federal Reserve's target of less than 10 percent for M-2 and less than 9 percent for M-1. At the time, Federal Reserve Chairman Paul Volcker said it was too early to worry about high rates of monetary growth since the measures of money supply reflected the new super money market accounts and money market demand accounts, distorting the old base from which money market growth had formerly been measured.

The following array of capital requirements makes an 8 to 10 percent rate of money growth likely in 1984:

- The Treasury needs to float at least $180 billion of new debt in fiscal 1984 to finance budget deficits and off-budget projects.
- The Treasury needs to borrow at least $600 billion in 1984 to refinance old debt.
- American corporations have $400 billion of debt, of which $40 billion to $80 billion must be turned into long-term debt.
- Individuals and families have a large pent-up demand for mortgage money.

Figure 1.

Money Supply (M-1, M-2),
1960-1983

Source: U. S. Department of Commerce

Note: M-1 includes currency outside the Treasury, Federal Reserve Banks and the vaults of commercial banks; demand deposits at all commercial banks; and foreign demand balances. M2 includes M1 plus time deposits at commercial banks.

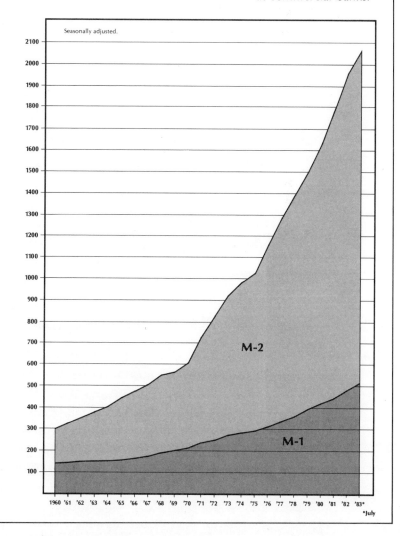

In addition, another important factor is effecting an increase in the money supply: the Federal Reserve is not requiring depository institutions to set aside reserves for money market demand accounts. This policy has released $3.5 billion of reserves, which could amount to $21 billion in new money, if a multiplier of six is used (which assumes a 16 percent reserve requirement) and assuming these monies remain in the banking system. To appreciate this sum, consider that $21 billion in new money would be enough to finance roughly a third of all homes to be built this year (assuming an average loan of $50,000).

According to the Federal Home Loan Bank Board, the new abundance of money has prompted savings and loan institutions (S&Ls) to return to making fixed-rate loans. Now 73 percent of their loans are at fixed rates, although just the reverse was true within the past year. Furthermore, the quasi-federal agencies known as Freddie Mac and Fannie Mae are buying up loans as fast as the S&Ls and banks can supply them. Since housing construction affects more sectors of the economy than any other industry, it is a fair assumption that the increased number of annualized housing starts in the second quarter of 1983 bodes well for the economy. Statistics for that quarter show between 1.5 and 1.7 million annualized units, compared to 1.1 million in 1982. Since it now appears that ample funds are available for financing new homes, there is reason to believe this sector will contribute to the growth of GNP and productivity through 1984.

UNUSED CAPACITY August 1983 saw U.S. businesses operating at only 71 percent of their industrial capacity; many businesses cut overhead by idling plants. Smokestack industries like steel and aluminum are operating at less than 50 percent capacity. With lower production costs per tonnage of steel and aluminum, the potential for an improved profit picture is substantial. And as the cost of money declines — it dropped 600 basis points between early 1982 and mid 1983 — many businesses again reach a point at which return on equity is acceptable. Since the capacity to produce is already in place, the return on incremental production goes straight to the bottom line.

In mid 1983 the return on equity of the 1,500 value line companies was only 7.8 percent. This rate of return on equity reflects operations at the tail end of a recession. It does not reflect the tremendous profits to come from lower costs of money, leaner management and production techniques, and the low costs of tapping unused capacity to meet expanding demand.

Clearly, one of the reasons the stock market acted so well in the first half of 1983 was anticipation of increased earnings. As public corporations' earnings improve, corporations are likely to have ample opportunity to raise more equity dollars through public offerings. This will further cut interest costs because, no doubt, some new equity dollars will be used to pay off existing expensive debt.

TAX AND INVESTMENT INCENTIVES Substantial personal tax reductions resulted from the $35 billion tax cut effective July 1983 (the third phase of the Economic Recovery Tax Act of 1981). The effects of the tax cut should be seen in increased savings as well as increased consumer spending. The maximum capital gains tax is now 20 percent (down from 28 percent). In addition, the individual retirement account (IRA) will continue to grow in popularity, particularly as people entering their peak earning years realize that they should not rely on future Social Security payments to provide for even the bare necessities during their retirement.

SAVINGS Since November 1982, Americans have been saving approximately 6 percent of their personal income. They have done so, in part, by not buying during the peak consumer buying season in the last quarter of 1982. Only in March and April 1983 did retail sales begin to exhibit strength. As the economy recovers, consumers will feel more at ease about spending. Since the savings rate in the past has averaged 3.5

percent of personal income, this period of low spending and high savings indicates enormous potential demand. The additional savings will provide the credit necessary to buy durable goods and homes.

THE ECONOMIC POWER OF A BULL MARKET In the 1970s many predicted that the Dow Jones industrial average would reach 2,000. But throughout the decade it bounced between 800 and 1,000 without ever showing any inclination to break out to the predicted heights. In August 1982, the Federal Reserve began to loosen the restraints on the money supply. At that time Henry Kaufman, chief economist for Salomon Brothers, reversed his prediction for interest rates, stating that he foresaw a substantial drop in short-term rates and a meaningful drop in long-term rates over the next twelve months. The stock market took off on a historic rise, climbing from a low in the 700s to reach all-time highs above 1,200 (see Figure 2). At the same time, bond prices began to rally dramatically, with most blue-chip bonds increasing in value by at least 25 percent.

A major bull market began in August 1982, and the Dow Jones average jumped approximately 60 percent in the ensuing twelve months. There are three primary reasons for today's great bull market trend: (1) investors' inflation expectations are lower; (2) they expect higher corporate earnings; (3) stocks do not yet have to compete with the high-yielding bonds and money market instruments, as they did between 1980 and mid 1982. If investors perceive that a dollar of earnings is worth a dollar of buying power and that the compounded rate of their stocks' earnings is growing, the bull market will continue as long as money market instruments and bonds do not appear to be a better alternative. When money market rates are high, many stockholders switch into money market instruments or tangibles such as real estate, expecting that real estate will grow at least as fast as inflation and will be taxed at capital gains rates.

The net result of the bull market has been to allow corporations and municipalities to float debt for longer

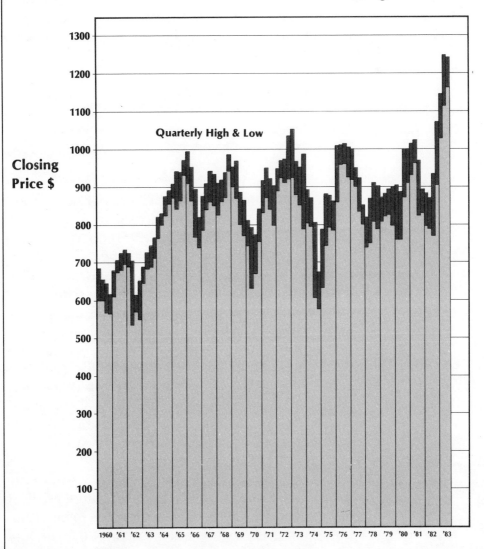

Figure 2.

Dow-Jones Industrial Average,
1960-1983

Source: Standard & Poor's Statistical Service

*Note: The Dow-Jones Indus-
trial Average repre-
sents the closing com-
posite price of thirty
leading industrial stocks.*

**Closing
Price $**

Quarterly High & Low

periods of time at rates that are 200 to 300 basis points lower than those prevailing in 1981 and early 1982. In addition, corporations' ability to issue equity has been enhanced. In six of the last seven recessions since World War II, a bull market led the general recovery by three to six months.

As equity investing becomes more attractive, economic recovery is secured. Equity capital provides businesses the opportunity to expand, experiment, develop, and even make mistakes without the pressures of an expensive debt burden. Further, equity capital enables businesses to pay off the expensive debt they acquired during the period of higher interest rates. If a corporation's debt structure is more expensive than its return on equity, it will realize immediate earnings growth simply by paying off that debt. For this reason, if interest rates remain fairly stable and equity capital continues to be available, corporate earnings should look very good well into 1984.

CONSUMER CONFIDENCE AND OPTIMISM

As corporate earnings continue to improve, so will the psychological atmosphere, which further helps accelerate economic recovery. In mid 1982, the University of Michigan Survey Research Center reported that the consumer confidence index (which indicates consumers' willingness to spend) had fallen below 50 percent. Subsequent reports show that confidence jumped to over 90 percent in mid 1983. And the index is expected to advance to 95 percent, a fifteen-year high. The consumer confidence index usually anticipates actual spending by two to three months, but retail volume rose 1.6 percent in April, on top of a revised 1.7 percent increase in March (the original March estimate was 0.3 percent). This evidence all shows the consumer spending mood as turning very positive.

One reason consumers have a sense of wealth is the increase in value of their equity investments. If 50 million people each perceive themselves to be $1,000 richer, and each spends only a tenth of that amount, $5 billion of additional spending would take place.

12

Consumer confidence indices lead us to expect a strong economic recovery — strong unless the Federal Reserve, fearing renewed high inflation, institutes a restrictive monetary policy. The second-longest peacetime boom (59 months) took place after the 1973–1975 recession, and in the later stages of the boom, the Federal Reserve had to step in to slow the momentum of inflation. Fortunately, there is no need for the Fed to take such action when the structural inflation rate is low (3 to 4 percent).

As the recovery matures, an increase in demand for funds by both the federal government and credit-worthy borrowers in the private sector could easily force interest rates up. To prevent a rate surge, the federal government should continue to strive for a balanced budget, even if it means raising taxes in 1984. For the time being, however, the recovery is moving like a locomotive that is just getting started.

We can gain some perspective on the consumption of REAL INTEREST RATES debt during the recent period of record borrowing rates if we look at real interest rates. The *real interest rate* is the difference between the cost of money and the concurrent rate of inflation. At the point of peak nominal interest rates in 1980, the annualized monthly rate of inflation averaged 13.5 percent (and peaked at 18 percent) with significant expectations among lenders that inflation could easily go higher. Thus, as the prime reached new highs, the real interest rate was also setting records (see Figure 3).

Today, the annual inflation rate has dropped to 3 to 4 percent. The cost of borrowing money is approximately 10.5 percent, roughly two to three times the real interest rate of the 1970's and before. In 1981, our economy was indeed in dire straits and the real rate of interest was understandably high. Now recovery is underway and economic prospects are bright, yet the real rate of interest is still much higher than the traditional 2 to 4 percent that held through the 1970's. This

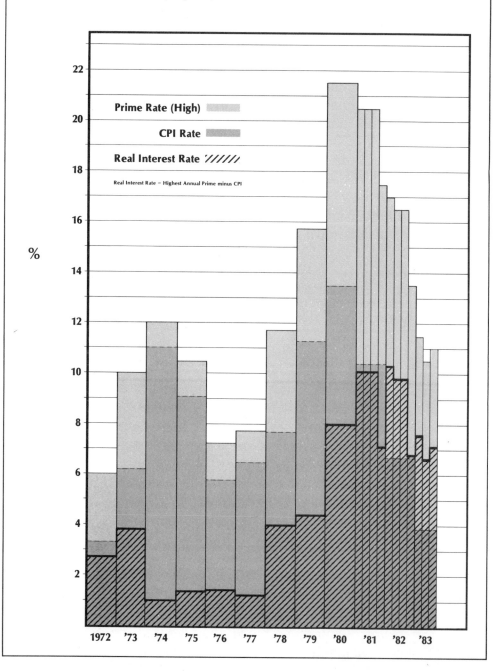

Figure 3.

Real Interest Rates,
1972-1983

Sources: U. S. Department of Commerce
Thorndike Encyclopedia, 1983 Yearbook

Prime Rate (High)

CPI Rate

Real Interest Rate ///////

Real Interest Rate = Highest Annual Prime minus CPI

%

22

20

18

16

14

12

10

8

6

4

2

1972 '73 '74 '75 '76 '77 '78 '79 '80 '81 '82 '83

curious situation exists because demand for capital is keeping the real cost of borrowing high.

Interest rates are determined by many factors. Among the most important are: (1) supply and demand for money, (2) the U.S. Treasury's need to finance its spending, (3) the Federal Reserve's policy regarding money supply, (4) the Federal Reserve's attitude toward pegging interest rates, and (5) borrower and lender expectations concerning inflation. Another significant factor is that bankers have become more ambitious in their pricing. During the recent period of record inflation bankers revised their traditional assumptions about inflation and discarded the rule of thumb used in the 1970s: that real interest rates should be pegged at 3 percent. Now, even though the rate of inflation has dropped dramatically, bankers have retained their expectations about long-term inflation, and they feel fully justified in charging real interest rates well above 3 percent. Bankers also believe they need additional yield to offset the losses they absorbed from bad loans during the recent recession, and to protect themselves against a renewed onslaught of double-digit inflation that could result from the economy overheating.

Will real rates of interest continue to be high in the foreseeable future? I believe they will unless bankers and savers are motivated to again revise their expectations concerning inflation. One stimulus would be to encourage savings by giving savers a tax break. This policy would effectively attack inflation by increasing investment, which should ultimately result in higher productivity. In Japan interest from savings is tax-free, and the supply of investment capital is ample because the Japanese save 18 percent of their personal income. Americans, in contrast, have traditionally saved less than 5 percent.

I propose that at least the first $1,000 of interest from a bank or savings and loan account be tax-free; and let up to 50 percent of the next $4,000 of interest paid by depository institutions be tax-free. This policy would encourage both personal savings and consumer spending, produce lower interest rates to borrowers, and provide the necessary capital for equipment, plant, and industrial expansion. These actions would, in turn, move us toward our national economic goals of full employment, high productivity, and affordable credit.

HIGHER INTEREST RATES: A MACROECONOMIC BLESSING

As we have seen, the old rules relating interest rates to inflation don't hold anymore. Lenders don't have to entice borrowers by making money cheap. Too many corporations must borrow just to avoid defaulting on earlier loans. Such pressure maintains higher rates.

While it may not seem so to the individual borrower, high interest rates will ultimately be seen as a blessing in disguise because they will result in a stronger dollar and a stronger economy. How can high interest rates, which are causing current hardships for many, achieve these boons? Consider the following analysis.

Inflation has been reduced in the past two years primarily by means of a well-monitored tightening of credit. The Federal Reserve's recent focus on money growth rather than interest rates has resulted in the availability of loan funds only at very high rates. In the international financial community, the Fed's shift in focus had critical consequences. Until the Fed changed its monetary policy, the dollar was taking a beating in foreign markets, gold reached $850 an ounce and, at one point, merchants in Europe hesitated to take the dollar at the morning exchange rate for fear that it would be much lower by evening. Since the dollar is the international trading currency, a run on the dollar creates economic chaos. Companies that accepted dollars without proper hedges in the futures market faced the threat of seeing their profits wiped out by a dollar devaluation.

Under the new Fed policy, interest rates climbed. Gold then dropped because investors preferred risk-free, high-yielding treasury instruments, at rates between 12 and 16 percent, to gold. Money was thus quickly poured out of gold and into money markets.

The recent high interest rates do pose a tremendous burden to small struggling businesses and to young couples desiring to buy a first home. But consider the following benefits of high interest rates on a macro-economic level, and whether they might not offset the difficulties faced by individuals.

- Fears have been allayed that the Fed was not acting responsibly to monitor our money supply. Renewed confidence has strengthened the dollar and arrested the run on gold.

- Corporations found borrowing too expensive to be justified unless they were certain of a high rate of return on their borrowed capital. This increased productivity and efficiency in business.

- Many prospective borrowers held off borrowing and waited for interest rates to descend. The economy consequently slowed, and reduced demand for funds caused interest rates to decline.

- Tight control of the money supply and general cutbacks throughout the economy contributed to the inflation rate dropping from 12 to 14 percent to its current 4 to 5 percent.

- Consumer debt has contracted significantly, and the resulting reservoir of consumer buying power will help stimulate the economy when consumer expectations are rosier.

The point is simply that high interest rates are not necessarily in themselves bad. They are, in fact, a mixed blessing, with salutary macroeconomic effects accompanied by microeconomic hardships. (We will return to the question of easing the hardships on individuals in Chapter 2 with a proposal for a two-tier interest-rate system.)

Chapter Two

The Global
Economy in 1984

Five years ago smart Americans looked abroad for investment opportunities. Buying into the Japanese or German stock market made great sense. Trading other currency for yen, marks, or Swiss francs was considered the better part of wisdom. Another leading school of thought held that exchanging any currency, even the yen or the mark, for gold or silver, was a shrewd play.

While this made sense in the short term, events of the past five years have shown such ideas were hardly the stuff of tactical economics. For the speculator or trader, the kind of person who sits on the floor of an exchange all day, they were great for a while. Even for the seasoned amateur who likes to play around with foreign currencies or commodities, there was a significant return. But for those who held on to these investments, the outcome has been poor to dismal.

Today foreign currencies, particularly the franc and the mark, are hurting. Gold, sold as the anchor of our monetary system, has dropped from $875 to $400 an ounce. Silver has gone from $38 to $12 an ounce. And even Japan, the only nation showing substantial sustained growth over the past five years, has seen a declining growth rate. These changes put the lie to the recent argument that America was not a safe harbor for investors.

Just a few years ago the flight from the dollar, a recessionary American economy, energy crisis, uncontrolled money supply at home, and lack of investment in our own plants and equipment, persuaded many investors to look abroad. And while it is true that we lost a share of the world trade market to Japan,

Germany, France, Taiwan, South Korea and other third-world nations, our economy has strengthened significantly during the past year.

Recently investors have reevaluated opportunities in America. The decline in the price of gold and silver, annual inflation in the consumer price index of less than 4 percent and a 20 percent rise in the dollar against all major currencies (except the Japanese yen) since January 1981 (see Figure 4), are three important factors in this turnaround.

All these events have occurred in a period in which the Federal Reserve has been pursuing a tight money policy. Concurrent events include: an unemployment rate of approximately 10 percent; interest rates, both long-term and short-term, below the recent all-time highs; an economy, as measured by the leading economic indicators, that is relatively flat but beginning a recovery; and two of America's largest industries, automotive and housing, still in the doldrums.

Why is it, then, that despite such tepid economic news the U.S. dollar is strong, the stock market has held its recent gains, the price of gold is one-half its recent high, and foreign investment in America is greater than ever before? The answer is that some kinds of negative news are very positive for an economy whose main problem is viewed to be inflation. The international financial and business community has never doubted America's ability to produce goods and services and to be innovative. Nor has that community ever lost faith in America's free-enterprise system or its world leadership in agricultural production and in many areas of technology and science. What did erode confidence in America and the dollar was our inability to control inflation.

Only in the last quarter of 1980 did the business community realize that the Federal Reserve was serious in its intention to restrict growth in the money supply to 3.5 to 6 percent as measured by M-1B (all currency, checking accounts, and NOW accounts). Through the first six months of 1980, the Fed, in fact, did keep the money supply under control, although the weekly supply bounced up and down erratically. To do so, the Federal Reserve maintained the federal funds rate (the rate that banks charge other banks for overnight loans) at historically high rates, on some days even hitting more than 20 percent. Further, the Fed's unwillingness to pump reserves into the banking system maintained a prime rate that hovered around 19 to 21 percent.

The Fed's effort was clearly designed to cool the economy. As the economy cooled, the inflation rate dropped and interest rates fell (although still high by historical standards), and inflation expectations have decreased, thus creating momentum for even lower inflation rates. Thus, negative indicators were positive for the long-term health of both the economy and the dollar.

INTERNATIONAL INVESTMENT

Current world economics may well mean that, for foreigners and Americans alike, equities in American business and American income-producing real estate are the best investment opportunities in the world today. Further, the cost of government as a percentage of GNP is substantially lower in the United States than in countries such as England, France, and Germany. Another attractive feature is the stability of the American political system.

It is no wonder, then, that European and Japanese investment in the United States is at an all-time high. It has more than doubled over the last five years, and the current trend indicates that it will repeat that performance in the next five years. For example, Japanese, French, British, and Canadian investors and companies are not only buying American home-building companies but are also starting new home-building companies in the U.S. because they recognize that the profit potential in that industry here is enormous compared to opportunities in their homelands. Home building is just one industry in which foreign investors have an interest. Such well-known American names as Howard Johnson Co., Union Bank, Crocker Bank, Fidelity Union Life Insurance Company, Bache Group, Inc., General Growth Properties Real Estate Investment Trust (REIT), Connecticut General Mortgage REIT, and a host of others have all either been subjects of takeover bids or have actually been taken over by foreign companies. In the last year alone, more than sixty banks in America were started or taken over by foreign interests, and it's a rare day when a major newspaper or financial journal doesn't run at least one story about a foreign company coming to the United States to do business.

When the value of the dollar is appreciating, yet another benefit accrues to foreign companies holding investments in the United States. When they take home their earnings in the form of dollars, they may be able to make a currency-exchange profit on top of their business profit. In turn, the collective foreign interest in America exerts an obvious, positive effect on the dollar's value: when foreigners exchange their currency for dollars in order to invest in America, the dollar appreciates. For example, an incremental billion dollars bought on the foreign exchange could significantly move the dollar up in a day's trading. At the same time, foreign equity-investment in the United States, to the extent it is used to start new businesses, creates new jobs and new products for Americans. Even though foreign investment in U.S.-based businesses sends dollars of profit to foreign countries, the U.S. benefits continue to multiply as salaries paid to American workers are deposited in American banks and thus provide future investment capital for other American ventures (Figure 4).

THE DOLLAR BOOM IS LIKELY TO CONTINUE Currently, the political trend in the United States is away from welfarism and socialistic tendencies. In Europe, it's just the opposite and various conditions tend to discourage foreign capital. The French have a socialist coalition government, which is expected to

24

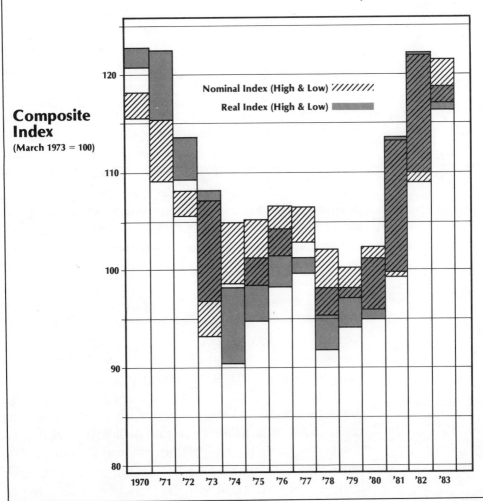

Figure 4.

Value of U. S. Dollar, Composite Foreign Exchange Rate,
1977-1983

Source: Morgan Guaranty Trust

Note: *Composite index is based on fifteen foreign currencies, which include the Canadian dollar, Japanese yen, British pound, West German mark, French franc and Swiss franc. Nominal rates are unadjusted; real rates are adjusted for inflation.*

Composite Index
(March 1973 = 100)

Nominal Index (High & Low) ////////.
Real Index (High & Low) ▬▬▬

120

110

100

90

80

1970 '71 '72 '73 '74 '75 '76 '77 '78 '79 '80 '81 '82 '83

further nationalize and regulate industry. The Scandinavian countries are all maintaining the status quo or implementing even more socialistic policies; Britain's socialistic economy has rendered her noncompetitive in many markets, and recent attempts at a turnaround have not been overly successful; Italy is struggling to maintain stability in its government and economy, with both unemployment and inflation on the rise; and West Germany is constantly threatened by the communist bloc to the East. Japan has cultural, legal, and geographical limitations that restrict foreign investment. In addition, both West Germany and Japan are extremely vulnerable to any crisis that would curtail oil shipments. Even Australia, which used to be considered the last of the great frontiers for investment, is discouraging foreigners from obtaining controlling interests in certain industries. Finally, although third-world nations would appear to present great investment opportunities, their political instability poses even greater risks.

Given the investment environment in other developed countries, it is not surprising that the United States has recently had an enormous increase in foreign investment, a trend that is likely to continue in the foreseeable future. The present investment climate is politically attractive, and there is no significant aversion to foreign interests' gaining control of businesses in even such sensitive areas as banking, insurance, or securities. Although high long-term interest rates will probably be with us through 1984 and into 1985, short-term rates could fluctuate dramatically. Because high long-term rates, which reflect lenders' and borrowers' inflation expectations, discourage borrowing, the economy will continue to drag a bit. This sluggishness will tend to restrain union wage contract and corporate profit expectations. And these diminished expectations will allow the rate of increase in prices to continue to fall, that is, the rate of inflation will continue to come down. In the meantime, continuing high yields on U.S. Treasury instruments and bank certificates of deposit will be extremely attractive to foreign investment. All these conditions will keep the dollar strong.

Also contributing substantially to a positive outlook for the U.S. economy is the fact that the U.S. now is importing significantly less oil than it was in 1979. It is no wonder that the prices of "scarce" commodities such as gold and silver have dropped precipitously. Although no one knows at what price gold will ultimately come to rest, one thing is certain: those who mine gold can do so profitably at prices significantly below $400 an ounce.

The continuing influx of foreign capital can be expected to push even higher the prices of U.S. stocks, real estate, and private companies, as the aggregate demand for these investments will continue to be high. Many good investment opportunities are now available to American investors who know where to look. Consider, for example, the stocks of companies that are logical merger candidates. These include companies whose price per share is significantly below book value and companies that are cash rich with low price/earnings multiples.

HOW CAN AMERICAN INVESTORS CAPITALIZE ON THE CURRENT SCENARIO?

In a recent study (called "Tobin's Q"), the Council of Economic Advisors reported on the market value of American public corporations expressed as a percentage of their replacement cost. High inflation and high corporate tax rates have manifested current market prices substantially below replacement cost — and bargains for investors.

	Market Value as Percentage of Replacement Cost
1960	0.956
1965	1.250
1970	0.863
1972	1.012
1974	0.663
1976	0.740
1978	0.602
1980	0.526

Americans can also consider investing in syndications that are buying large, quality real estate projects which would qualify for sale to American and foreign buyers. Other opportunities include growth industries such as petrochemicals, biomedical technology, computers (both hardware and software), mini-robots, defense, and a host of others. Given the atmosphere for tax incentives and other forms of encouragement intended to increase American productivity, now is also a good time to buy into *small* companies in growth industries. These small firms, too, are excellent merger candidates in an environment that seems to foster merger fever.

If stocks continue to rise and cash remains king, more buy-outs will involve stock trades and fewer will involve cash. The advantage here is that stock trades are tax deferred; therefore, all parties benefit. The buying party retains its cash, and the selling party defers taxes. In addition, it is not unusual for the selling company's stockholders to receive a premium of 50 to 100 percent over the stock price prior to the merger. Recent attractive mergers from the selling stockholders' position include:

Acquiring Company	*Selling Company*
Shell Oil	Belridge Oil Co.
Fluor Corp.	St. Joe Minerals Corp.
Standard Oil (Ohio)	Kennecott
RCA Corp.	C.I.T. Financial Corp.
Kraft, Inc.	Dart Industries
Union Pacific Railroad	Missouri Pacific
Nabisco, Inc.	Standard Brands Foods Div.
Cooper Industries	Crouse-Hinds Co.
Marmon Group, Inc.	Trans Union Financial Corp.
Tenneco Chemicals, Inc.	Southwestern Life Ins. Co.
Wheelabrator-Frye, Inc.	Pullman, Inc.
Cooper Industries	Gardner-Denver Co.
American Brands, Inc.	FDS Holding
Getty Oil	Reserve Oil, Inc.

Real estate is another source of good investment opportunities. While the prices of recent property sales seem high by historical standards, they still could be considered cheap on a depreciated replacement-cost basis (replacement cost less accumulated depreciation). Foreign and institutional demand for American real estate continues to be strong. In recent years, Canadian, German, Dutch, French, and Japanese investors' purchases of American income-producing real estate have accelerated. In addition, major pension plans are expected to invest approximately 1 percent of their assets, or $6 billion, in real estate within the next two years. Their interests in real estate are projected to soar to $80 billion, or 10 percent of their expected assets, within five years.

In addition to the foreign and institutional demand, recent changes in the tax laws will encourage more people to invest in quality real estate projects. Two of the most salient features of the new tax laws are: (1) the reduction of maximum tax on unearned income from 70 to 50 percent, which effectively reduces maximum capital gains tax from 28 to 20 percent; and (2) new rules that allow the depreciation of certain kinds of real estate over fifteen years. This latter provision alone can triple the tax benefits on certain kinds of real estate, according to one accounting firm.

Since most real estate investors expect capital gains, it is not surprising that their interest should be stimulated by the new tax laws. These new laws and the foreign and institutional investment markets should provide ample demand for quality real estate projects purchased by syndicators. Today investors of moderate means can enjoy the fruits of this environment by investing with professional syndicators who have the expertise and capital base to choose and manage projects that only the very rich could hope to own before large syndication offerings became available to the public.

WHAT COULD GO WRONG?

While the economic outlook seems positive for at least the next twenty-four months, any one of a number of crises could overturn this prediction. It is not difficult to compose a long list of international events any one of which could seriously disrupt the world economy: an OPEC boycott, a worldwide drought, renewed Russian aggression, a holy war in the Mid-

East, a rampage of terrorist attacks, or the default of several less-developed countries (LDCs). However, I prefer to think positively, firmly believing that mankind will continue to resist self-destruction. An individual who lives as if the world were coming to an end is part of the problem instead of the solution. Furthermore, if everyone were to hoard gold and silver as a hedge against catastrophe, there would be no investment capital to continue our quest to improve our stay on earth. Gold and silver hidden in the basement do not produce a thing. And while investments in commodities such as gold and silver probably make good sense as long-term hedges against inflation, the real excitement in the next twenty-four months will, I believe, be in other areas — real estate and the stock market — right here in the U.S.

In my view, the best investment in the world today is owning U.S. dollars and investing those dollars in well-chosen U.S. stocks and improved U.S. real estate. That current prices are a bargain, when compared to depreciated replacement cost, will, I think, become continuously more apparent to investors here at home and abroad. I believe that no currency will be as strong as the U.S. dollar for the next twenty-four months, and that no investment opportunity will offer the same stability and risk/reward ratio as those equities available in the United States.

As Europe comes out of its recession, the U.S. economy will only get stronger. All our free economic system needs is a positive economic environment in which to operate. That environment is now developing and will improve as it becomes apparent to our government's leaders that the economy is again becoming healthy.

The current momentum convinces me that now is the time to invest in American industry and American improved real estate — at prices that will look like bargains compared to the prices twenty-four months from now.

Chapter Three

Gold:
Magic Metal,
A Good Investment
or Just Another
Commodity?

Should a revolution or civil disorder ever lead to a national apocalypse, most of us, investment experts included, would naturally be preoccupied with the welfare of friends and family. Insuring their safety and trying to restore peace will surely be the order of the day. But some farsighted investors believe the only thing that can insure their "safe passage" is gold. I've wondered for some time about these doomsday speculators. Do they plan to approach barricaded supermarkets and talk their way into the frozen food department by flashing Krugerrands or Canadian Maple Leafs? Despite what these theorists suggest there is nothing miraculous about gold, in good or bad times.

I've never thought panic was a good reason to buy anything. Gold is just another commodity. If, as these worry warts suggest, we are headed toward an economic collapse, it seems obvious that a reliable source of food and daily necessities would be far more valuable than fifty ounces of gold. I never tell clients they must invest one way or another. Advisors are precisely what the word implies: people who provide information to help you make up your own mind. You should never do something on the simple say so of consultants because sooner or later someone will give you bad advice. What's important is that you analyze any advice in light of your experience and then make up your own mind.

Having said all that I would like to go on record, here and now, with one caveat: try to avoid making investments because you think western civilization is going to collapse. There are a lot of variables in tactical investing, but I guarantee you precious metals are not going to be your salvation during a revolution.

The very fact that it's necessary to make this point suggests the degree of myth surrounding gold.

Gold has been used for ornamental purposes and monetary exchange for more than 4,000 years. Gold is durable, pliable, attractive to the eye, and relatively scarce. Yet gold has never been thought of as truly indispensable to mankind's progress.

Gold fans are quick to point out its price has always kept pace with inflation. In 1940, when gold was $35 an ounce, a man could buy a suit for $35; and in 1979, when gold was $300 an ounce, one could also buy a man's suit for $300.

My opinion is that if an investment does no more than keep up with inflation, it leaves something to be desired. I like investments to do considerably better than inflation, unless risk avoidance is the investor's main criterion. Simply put, investors cannot increase their real net worth unless the after-tax rate of return on their investments surpasses the inflation rate.

Over the last six years gold's performance as an investment commodity has been both spectacular and erratic. In 1976, it touched $100 an ounce before rising as high as the $870 range in 1980; but during the first half of 1983 its price hovered between $420 and $490.

Studies of various commodities show that equally speculative commodities have outperformed gold. For example, silver doubled in price between June 1982 and February 1983, but gold went up only 50 percent during the same period (see Figure 5). And the actual performance of gold as a long-term investment has been lackluster. It has increased in value from $35 an ounce in 1935 to its present value of roughly $400 an ounce, a compounded growth rate of 5.7 percent a

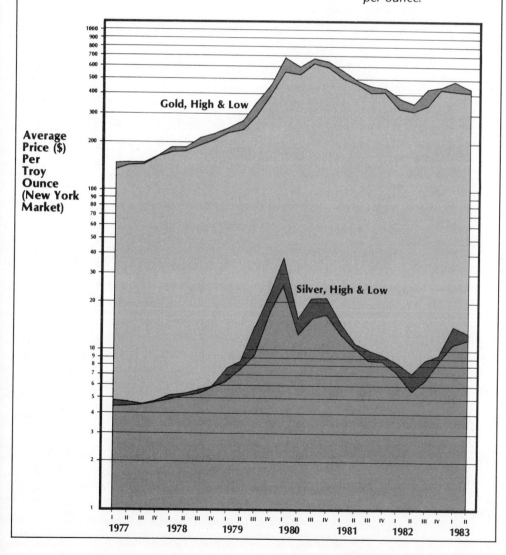

Prices of Gold & Silver,
1980-1983

Figure 5.

Source: Standard & Poor's Current Statistics

Note: Prices represent average for fiscal quarter.
In early 1980, gold
briefly soared to over
$800 per ounce on the
London market; con-
currently, silver hit its
historic high: $38.27
per ounce.

**Average
Price ($)
Per
Troy
Ounce
(New York
Market)**

Gold, High & Low

Silver, High & Low

1000
900
800
700
600
500
400
300
200
100
90
80
70
60
50
40
30
20
10
9
8
7
6
5
4
3
2
1

I II III IV   I II III IV   I II III IV   I II III IV   I II III IV   I II III IV   I II
1977   1978   1979   1980   1981   1982   1983

year. While it is true that gold's value was long fixed at the $35-an-ounce exchange rate promised by the United States government, it is also true that the correction in the gold price since the early 1970s (when the U.S. effectively went off the gold standard) would have to have been much greater than the present $400-an-ounce price if gold is to be considered an extraordinary long-term investment.

WHAT IS THE TRUE WORTH OF GOLD?

Gold is worth whatever a buyer will pay a seller, given reasonable time to make a decision. Intrinsically, gold does not have any more value than any other commodity or service. An example of this principle was seen in Germany in 1923, when German currency was not worth the paper it was printed on. Individuals who did not hold any gold could easily obtain goods and services by trading other goods and services. Further, while holders of gold were in a good trading position, holders of silver, sterling, foreign currencies, antiques, art, and other forms of property were also able to obtain the necessities. It is interesting to note that when Americans were finally allowed to buy gold, for the first time in more than thirty-five years, gold actually dropped in price.

GOLD AND THE GLOBAL ECONOMY

Problems with gold-backed currencies caused nations to "float" their currencies; that is, no nation is now willing to guarantee the redemption of its currency for gold. In the 1950s and 1960s, when the U.S. had in excess of 20 percent of the world's exports, there was a good reason for backing the dollar with gold, particularly since most world trade was conducted in terms of dollars. Today, however, U.S. dominance in world markets has declined: the combined Common Market countries and Japan export as much or more than the U.S. If these nations can continue to expand their exports without glorifying gold, they are unlikely to revert to gold-backed currencies since to do so would bring no benefit, only the distasteful restriction as to how much money their nations' treasuries can print.

Some theoretical economists have suggested that the major trading nations might develop an international trading currency backed by gold contributed by those nations. The mid-Eastern oil-producing countries, for example, might feel more comfortable holding such supercurrency instead of dollars.

How would such a supercurrency work? To start with, it is unlikely to be backed by more than 10 percent gold reserves. As one nation's currency weakened, it would be required to ante up more gold reserves, but it would probably not have the gold to contribute. It could borrow gold from other nations with stronger currency, but those nations might hesitate to respond to such a request. Why would they hesitate? Because to lend a weak nation more gold would mean not only accepting that weak nation's deficit trade balance but also in effect underwriting its ability to incur further deficit. At that point gold would start to break down as a backing for currencies, since the gold-holding nations would always be contributing a disproportionate amount of gold for the benefit of those whose gold reserves were low.

The prime stimulus to a gold-backed supercurrency would be if the oil-producing (OPEC) nations demanded gold or a gold-backed currency for their oil. But the current oil glut makes that an unlikely prospect. Furthermore, although some OPEC nations are buying gold, others are more cautious. For example, the finance minister of Kuwait (the fourth largest producer of oil, behind Saudi Arabia, Iran, and Iraq) once claimed that gold was not an answer to his country's economic security. Rather, he stressed ownership in diversified businesses as the key to economic health. His stance reflects the simple recognition that on the day when there is no more oil, the income necessary to provide for Kuwait's people must come from diversified industries. Looking toward that day, Kuwait purchased a 25 percent interest in Daimler-Benz in Germany and has also purchased real estate and other business interests in the U.S.

The Common Market nations, Japan, and the U.S. have all taken the position that it is not in their interest to view gold as anything other than a commodity. It is logical for them to take this position, since both creditor and debtor nations are vulnerable should gold take on new monetary significance. Creditor nations would be vulnerable because their trading surpluses could become less valuable, and the debtor nations would be vulnerable because their currency could be devalued, making debt retirement more expensive.

Are there tools other than gold that might more effectively create monetary stability? In forming the International Monetary Fund (IMF) and the World Bank, nations cooperated to facilitate expansion of world commerce and the abandonment of protectionist trade policies. The system has worked for nearly four decades to prevent monetary chaos, and it is reasonable to assume it will continue to do so in the foreseeable future. In the final analysis, the valuation system that will work is the one nations can agree on. Fiat money (i.e., debits and credits in central bank accounts) is as essential for world commerce as airplanes and cargo ships. Currency values artificially tied to gold do not have the flexibility necessary for today's world economy.

Nations must constantly and diligently cooperate to maintain international commercial stability. An example of such cooperation to maintain a stable commercial environment was Germany and Japan's $30 billion support package to stabilize the dollar against the yen and the Deutsche mark in November 1978. Their cooperation was in part motivated by their own national interests in not allowing the value of a major trading partner's currency to drop too low. Communication and cooperation among governments and banks are in fact much more important to a stable world economy than gold could ever be.

CAN GOLD STABILIZE THE DOLLAR?

Exporting nations rejoice when the dollar gets stronger. When that happens, countries with strong currencies, such as Japan, Germany, and Switzerland, find their exports much more competitive in the world market. Similarly, when the dollar becomes weaker, their exports become more expensive, and thus less competitive compared with those of U.S. manufacturers. Furthermore, a weakening dollar encourages inflation in the U.S. because trading partners raise prices to compensate for the declining dollar. Thus, it is to our economic advantage to have a relatively stable dollar that does not experience great swings in value. Can a gold standard accomplish this?

The answer is no. The true value of the U.S. dollar is determined by factors such as the U.S. trade surplus or deficit, the increase in money supply, and real interest rates (the difference between the cost of borrowing money and the current rate of inflation). A stable U.S. dollar can be accomplished by restraint in expanding the national money supply and by an increase in productivity. Since we went off the gold standard, world commerce has dramatically expanded. In 1973, when currencies began to float freely, the most productive nations benefited, and the least productive were penalized. This is understandable; in fact, any other result would prove the system is not working. Inflation occurs when a country prints money at a rate faster than its growth in productivity; its currency is devalued. This decline in value occurs whether there is a gold standard or not. To attempt to artificially maintain value for a currency by backing it with gold is an exercise in futility.

GOLD IS A COMMODITY

Gold is a commodity that has had a strong surge in the marketplace. While it has been time-tested over forty centuries, gold has its limitations as a thing of value. The attractiveness of gold includes its bright color, malleability, durability, and relative scarcity. Those are nice qualities, but they do not necessarily make for a good investment.

In fact, if gold is not monetarized and remains at today's prices or higher, and supply and demand are not at an equilibrium, we may have a glut of gold in the marketplace in the next two or three years. No individual can accurately predict the potential supply of gold at today's prices.

As an investment, gold has some distinct disadvantages. It is hard to leverage, it does not produce income, it's speculative, and it can be expensive to store in volume. Why, then, do people invest in gold? Gold can always be a good "safe passage commodity" if one needs resources to escape a country; it can be used for hiding one's wealth; and it is likely to keep pace with inflation. But gold's many limitations prevent it from ever being the sole answer to the conservative investor's security.

An investor who feels a need to enjoy the benefits of gold ownership might consider maintaining between 10 and 20 percent of his or her investment portfolio in gold. But people who are seeking to convert all their assets into gold are making a mistake because they're depriving themselves of income opportunities available in real estate, the stock market, business, and even high-yielding, short-term fixed money instruments. While gold is shiny, bright, and beautiful to look at, it is still just another commodity. It will probably increase in value over the long term but will also have severe ups and downs in between.

Chapter
Four

The Great
Gold Gamble

If you're eager to put 10 to 20 percent of your portfolio into gold, make sure you consider the risks before you dream about the benefits. While gold prices are likely to drift upward over the next two years, expect great fluctuations along the way. The fact is there are convincing scenarios suggesting that gold could go up or down as much as 40 percent during the coming year. Clearly, this is not an investment for the faint hearted. Like any other speculative investment, gold gains in direct proportion to a variety of factors. They include:

- Expectations of high inflation.
- World political tension.
- Higher costs of mining.
- Increasing world economic problems.
- Insolvency of financial institutions.
- Increasing prospects for returning to a gold standard.
- Rates of return on competitive investment vehicles.
- Investors' increasing ability to speculate in the metal through various types of commodity exchanges.

Does this sound like the safe, secure investment touted by gold ads? The fact is that since early 1980, gold has fluctuated dramatically, at times wildly, falling more than 60 percent, then gaining 70 percent. Why did gold plunge from $875 an ounce in January 1980 to $295 in June 1982 and then bounce back to $493 in February 1983? One reason is that in the last quarter of 1981 and throughout most of 1982, money market yields were so high that it paid investors to take profits in gold and then invest safely in money market instruments. Gold holders became gold sellers. But when money market instruments no longer paid double-digit yields, investors moved back into gold. Hence the drop in value from 1980 through mid 1982, then the climb back as interest rates declined (see Figure 6).

WHAT LIES AHEAD FOR GOLD? It now appears that the balance of the eight factors mentioned above will direct gold prices upward over the next two years, but with great fluctuations along the way. The two most important factors are these: (1) international financial institutions are in jeopardy with debt overexposure in weak economies, that is, substantial portions of their loan portfolios are invested in nations whose economies have forced them to defer repayment, and (2) the economies of many of the world's industrial nations are showing signs of weakness.

In response to these two conditions, the major industrial nations may choose to monetize debt (print money) and thus provide banking institutions with the needed liquidity to offset defaulted debt and to stimulate the weak economies. In fact, this process has begun with the recent recommendation of the International Monetary Fund (IMF) that lesser-developed countries (LDCs) be issued additional special drawing rights (SDRs) in order to help pay off obligations incurred with major banks located in the major industrial nations. Countries allocated these SDRs can use them to pay off commercial bank lenders.

The irony of such a transaction is that the IMF does not have money to repay the new debt unless the lending nations donate capital. In effect, such a policy ultimately transfers the repayment of debt to the taxpayers of nations donating to the IMF. Thus, the bank owed money is ultimately paid off with money printed by the nation in which it is located. This is *foreign aid* without appearing as such in the federal budget, but the result is just as inflationary.

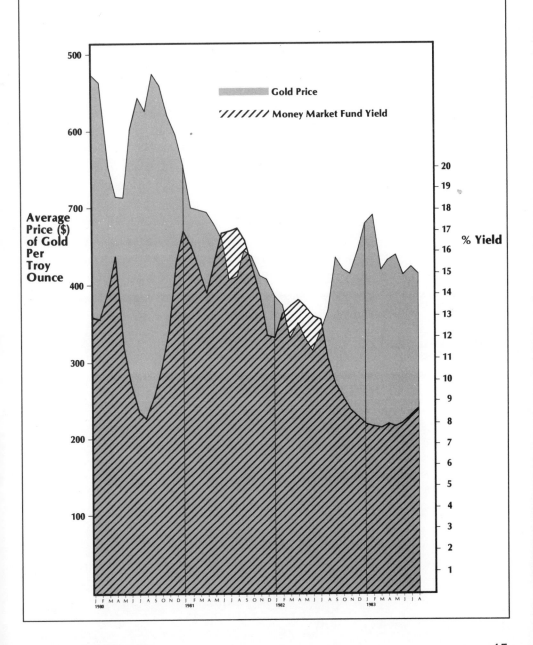

Figure 6.

Gold Prices &
Money Market Fund Yields,
1980-1983

Sources: Commodity Yearbook, 1983
Donoghue's Money Fund Report

Gold Price

Money Market Fund Yield

Average
Price ($)
of Gold
Per
Troy
Ounce

% Yield

500
600
700
400
300
200
100

20
19
18
17
16
15
14
13
12
11
10
9
8
7
6
5
4
3
2
1

J F M A M J J A S O N D J F M A M J J A S O N D J F M A M J J A S O N D J F M A M J J A
1980   1981   1982   1983

The U.S. Congress must approve any additional allocation to the IMF, and Federal Reserve Chairman Paul Volcker has recommended that at least $8.5 billion be contributed to the IMF to back the allocation of new SDRs. (As a matter of interest, the IMF has requested a total of $34 billion of new SDRs, with Volcker's recommended $8.5 billion representing the contribution of the U.S.) Since the federal budget typically does not include an allocation for special contributions to the IMF, Congressional approval could direct the Federal Reserve to create, out of thin air, $8.5 billion of additional capital to be contributed to the IMF for new SDRs.

If we print the additional money to prop up the LDCs and the lending banks, the value of gold should increase. And if we do not prop up the LDCs and bank insolvency results, there will be a rush to hard currency — that is, to gold — and the price of gold would again increase. How can this be? If Congress does not allow the Fed to print the $8.5 billion for the IMF, we put our largest banks in jeopardy because there is little chance they will be paid off by the debtor LDCs. However, if we print the money, we devalue our own currency. In either case, the result is to put additional upward pressure on the price of gold.

PROSPECTS FOR THE U.S. MONEY SUPPLY

There is an overwhelming vested interest in steady recovery from the 1981–1982 recession. It seems highly unlikely that the current administration will put any pressure on the Federal Reserve Board to further apply the brakes to the money supply. Indeed, the advent of new money market instruments offered by banks has left everyone unsure of how to measure the money supply. The Fed will need at least a year to analyze exactly what they should be monitoring: M-1, M-2, the monetary base, or some combination of two of these three. Some bank money market checking accounts are now included in M-1, and there is uncertainty as to what the starting base of M-1 should be. The money supply might grow at a far greater clip than normal without the Fed being able to measure it accurately.

Chairman Volcker informed Congress that it is now the Fed's intent to watch both interest rates and money supply so that interest rates remain in line with the overall state of the economy. In early stages of the recovery, the Fed could choose to relax a firm control on the money supply so as not to abort the recovery. The result of this relaxation could be inflationary in the coming year. Gold may fluctuate dramatically in response to money supply news, dropping in value as the economy begins to accelerate, then rising as inflation evidences itself.

Another factor affecting gold prices is how gold compares to investment alternatives. In this context, gold looks like a decent buy. Both the stock market and real estate, for example, are close to their all-time highs. Gold, at between $400 and $500 an ounce, is considerably under its January 1980 high of $875.

INVESTMENT RELATIVITY

When interest rates from money market instruments were as high as 16 percent, gold was not nearly as attractive as it is today. To match investments yielding 16 percent, gold would have to double in value every four and one-half years. However, when interest yields from money market instruments are about 8 percent, gold need only double every nine years to equal money market returns.

If gold were to rise from $500 to $700, a 40 percent increase, it would still be $175 below its all-time high. By comparison, if the Dow were to rise from 1,100 to 1,400, a 27 percent increase, it would represent a substantial breakout to a new historic high. The same analogy can be applied to real estate values. Therefore, from a psychological standpoint, gold looks like a reasonable buy, particularly if it drops to the $300 to $350 range.

In 1984 gold could plummet. The potential $75 billion deficit balance of trade for 1983 might provide incentive for the U.S. to offer credit to stimulate exports. However, these debts must be paid off with dollars. It is possible that in order to acquire dollars for

CAN THE PRICE OF GOLD DROP 40 PERCENT IN THE NEXT YEAR?

trade with the Western nations, the Soviet Union and Mid-Eastern countries will dump gold, driving the price of gold down.

Or interest rates could take off again, once more making gold appear to be an expensive metal to hold, especially if inflationary expectations remain low. The onset of high interest rates could prompt an upward spike in gold prices because the increased cost of borrowing money is initially viewed by most investors as inflationary. However, if rates remain high for a period of time their deflationary impact takes hold, and gold owners with waning inflationary expectations will sell.

Gold would also drop if the dollar gets stronger. Although this is possible, I do not believe it will occur in the next twelve months because the U.S. has to increase exports if we are to have a decent recovery. The dollar is now already too strong to support a favorable balance of trade. Our goods, compared to goods produced abroad, are too expensive. Since exports typically represent at least 20 percent of the gross national product (GNP), if the dollar were allowed to continue to rise, its strength would have a significant adverse effect on GNP growth.

Yet another potential depressor of gold prices is the oil glut. Cheap oil lowers inflationary expectations. As oil prices drop, more energy will be consumed, more people will be employed, the velocity of money's circulation will increase, and the money supply will expand to accommodate increasing industrial capacity. This cycle will lessen the attraction of gold compared to the stock market and real estate, which will outperform the inflation rate in the early stages of a growth economy.

CAN THE PRICE OF GOLD RISE 40 PERCENT IN THE NEXT YEAR? However, gold may go up. Lower oil prices created hardships on many small oil companies, manufacturers of drilling equipment, and small refineries. Because they borrowed heavily from lending institutions in ex-

48

pectation of higher oil prices, they now find themselves strapped into rolling over debt they cannot retire. Several smaller oil-producing nations that were counting on higher oil prices to pay off debts are in a similar situation. These nations' problems in repaying their loans have placed some U.S. financial institutions in jeopardy, which, as noted earlier, puts upward pressure on gold. Again, the West is likely to prop up its banks by printing more money and the inflationary impact of thus monetizing debt will stimulate gold to go up.

Also consider the distinct possibilities of heightened cold war anxieties; international political crises in the Mideast, Africa, and Central America; or significant deferments in international debt payment schedules. Any of these will cause gold to rise in value. Am I saying gold may go up or go down? Correct. Depending on which factor exerts the most influence at a given point in time, the mass psychology of fear and greed will push gold prices up *or* down.

WHAT IS THE SAFEST WAY TO BUY GOLD?

There is no safe way to buy gold because, as a heavily traded commodity, its price can fluctuate dramatically from day to day. The most speculative way to buy gold is to buy gold futures contracts. Since the investor puts down between only 5 and 10 percent of the value of the gold contract, he has enormous leverage, which can produce either large gains or large losses.

For the long term, a purchaser might do well to buy Krugerrands, pesos, maple leafs, or other gold coins for which the premium is no more than approximately 5 percent of the intrinsic troy value of the coin. This is wiser than buying collector coins at a high premium over intrinsic troy ounce value. Such collector coins must usually be bought at retail prices, but cannot later be sold at other than wholesale prices, unless the investor is an expert actively dealing in collector coins.

Risk-tolerant investors interested in gold for the short run can consider buying a gold-mining stock and then selling a *call* against the stock. Suppose you buy 500 shares of a gold-mining stock and simultaneously sell five calls at a strike price 10 to 15 percent above the current market price of the stock. The income you receive from the sale of the calls will cover your downside up to about 15 percent. By placing a stop order to sell the gold-mining stock before it reaches the break-even point, you can guarantee yourself against a large loss. If the gold stock should go up, on the other hand, it is likely that the call you have sold will be exercised, and you can sell out the stock at a price approximately 15 percent above what you paid for it. Combining that modest gain with the 15 percent return from the sale of the call, you could obtain an annualized return of 50 percent or more after commissions on a six-month call. The risk of such a strategy is that the gold-mining stock could drop in value — triggering your stop order and resulting in a loss — and then rise to a price that would cause the call to be exercised. You would then have to rebuy the stock at the higher price in order to deliver it to the holder of the call.

Risk-adverse investors should not contemplate such short-term trading strategies, but should make a long-term diversified investment by means of a mutual fund of gold stocks or an individual portfolio of gold stocks and other valuable commodity metals stocks. As a matter of interest, one mutual fund (International Investors) gained more than 1500 percent in fifteen years (1967–1982) and more than 830 percent in ten years (1972–1982). Most of the issues the fund held were South African gold stocks. Each investor, of course, has to decide which method is most compatible with his or her own resources and attitude toward risk.

CONCLUSION: FOLLOW THE BOUNCING BALL There are more reasons for gold to rise in the next year or two than there are for it to drop, but either way there will be fluctuations in price. Gold probably has a more attractive reward-risk ratio today than certain other investment alternatives but, because of the high potential for severe fluctuations in price, it should be clearly understood as a speculative investment.

I emphasize "speculative" because gold is often sold under the guise of being a "safety" investment, a kind of long-term purchase that will guarantee one's secure retirement. While gold has the makings of a potentially great investment over the next couple of years, its purchase definitely should be made from that 10 or 20 percent of a portfolio set aside for speculative investments.

Part
Two

Real Estate —
The Investment
for the mid 1980s

Chapter Five

Investment Opportunities in Multifamily Housing

Tactical investors are not dreamers. As we've seen in the previous two chapters on gold, many speculators are willing to take big risks because they hope to become filthy rich. It's true that you might score next month in the gold market. It's also true that next month you might find oil in your backyard. But tactical investors don't generally like to play long shots. That's what's nice about real estate.

From 20 years experience in real estate, I can tell you that multifamily housing has produced a steady return for hundreds of thousands of big and little investors. People have chosen it repeatedly because of its demonstrated superiority to other available opportunities. Can multifamily housing meet your personal investment objectives? To answer that question, consider its advantages over the next eighteen months. Specifically, look at these eight categories:

- Supply and demand for the product during the period of investment.
- Barriers to entry by competitors who could appropriate a market share or reduce prices.
- Special tax advantages that mitigate risk.
- Available leverage and personal risk entailed.
- Controllability of assets in the event of unfavorable outcomes.
- Availability of special information.
- Likelihood of government intervention that could affect profitability or markets.
- Likelihood of union intervention that could affect profitability.

What's particularly appealing about multifamily housing is that you don't need a degree from the Wharton School of Business to understand why it's such a comparatively good investment. We've seen how gold can be dramatically influenced by a variety of exotic factors. And anyone who has played the stock market can tell you that many issues perform poorly even when companies maintain or exceed their earnings growth. Tactical investors like multifamily housing because it performs well during periods of inflation. And continuing high demand for multifamily housing makes it a relatively safe investment.

REAL ESTATE, STOCKS, AND INFLATION

Real estate generally performs well during periods of inflation for three reasons. First, during periods of inflation it is difficult for builders to acquire construction loans because current rents do not justify the higher costs of building. Therefore, people with existing properties tend to benefit because they have little or no competition from new construction. Second, real estate is a necessity; many individuals and families need to live in apartments; some retail and service businesses must be in shopping centers; professionals need to be quartered in office buildings. Despite higher prices and rents, people must have places to live and work. Third, when stocks and bonds are not performing well during inflationary times, real estate tends to be the beneficiary, as more individual investors and institutional investors find real estate attractive and bid up its price. In the 1970s, institutional investors (large pension and profit-sharing plans) increased their real estate holdings by approximately 500 percent as a percentage of their total assets managed. While it was once common for investment advisors to recommend that only 5 percent of a large pension or profit-sharing plan's assets be in real estate, it is now not uncommon for as much as 20 percent of such portfolios to be in real estate assets.

In contrast, stocks do not always keep pace with inflation: during the 1970s, the average annual inflation rate was 8 percent, but the Dow Jones industrial index grew at a compounded growth rate of less than 6 percent. Why did this index fail to keep up with inflation? First, stocks represent an emotional investment; that is, they tend to react dramatically to uncertainty. There is no question that the 1970s were fraught with uncertainties brought on by the Vietnam War, the OPEC oil embargo, the Watergate fiasco, the devaluation of the dollar in 1972 (which followed two devaluations in 1971), wage and price controls in 1972, and, last but not least, high interest rates and high inflation rates.

Second, in contrast to real estate, stocks are not necessities; they represent investment opportunities whose value fluctuates with buyers' perceptions of whether the price/earnings (p/e) ratio is fair, whether the company has growth potential, and a host of other such variables. (The p/e ratio is simply the current price per share divided by earnings per share.) When a stock's p/e ratio is 15 and its earnings are growing at a 20 percent compounded rate, the earnings can double in three and a half years, but the value of the investor's stock can double *only* if the p/e ratio remains constant. But, of course, the stock can easily drop in value or just stay the same, especially if investors perceive that a p/e ratio of 15 results in too high a market price in inflationary times. That is, investors willing to pay 15 times earnings for a stock during periods of low inflation (3 percent to 4 percent), may be willing to pay only 7.5 times earnings if inflation jumps to 13 percent or 14 percent, because inflation will eat up at least half the buying power of those earnings in a three-to-four–year period. This is, in fact, what happened to the stock market in the last half of the 1970s all the way up through August 1982: many growth stocks with historical p/e ratios of 10 to 20 saw their ratios drop to between 5 and 10. In most cases the rate of earnings growth of these stocks did not decline — but investors' perceptions of the value of their stocks' earnings did.

Let us now return to our evaluation of investments in multifamily housing by considering supply and demand. Supply and demand studies are central to an investor's understanding of current economic reality. Supply and demand determine not only what to invest in, but also when, where, and for how long.

With a favorable demand/supply ratio — that is, one in which the demand exceeds the supply — a generally poor economic environment can, in fact, prove to be a good one for certain types of investments. Residential housing in the United States is an excellent case in point. Compared to historical prices, in the last five years existing housing appeared to be grossly overpriced. Investors who thought about housing prices in the past concluded that prices had become higher than they *should have been*. But investors who observed actual conditions — net housing starts and increases in household formation — could quantify the probable demand/supply ratio. They observed that the market has reached a point at which demand is elastic relative to prices; that is, people drop out of the market either because they've been priced out or because they've chosen to wait for lower prices. To own an interest in apartment dwellings today is probably prudent — people who are not buying homes have to live somewhere.

In fact, the supply of multifamily housing has declined drastically since 1972, when housing reached an all-time high of over 2.2 million annual housing starts and an additional 1 million mobile home starts (see Figure 7). As of July 1983 the total housing starts are roughly 1.7 million with only 600,000 in multifamily housing. At the same time, economists in the Department of Housing and Urban Development (HUD) tell us that roughly 2 million housing starts are needed in order to keep up with demand for new housing and to replace housing that has either been destroyed or condemned.

Naturally, when housing costs become prohibitive people do double up and young people remain in

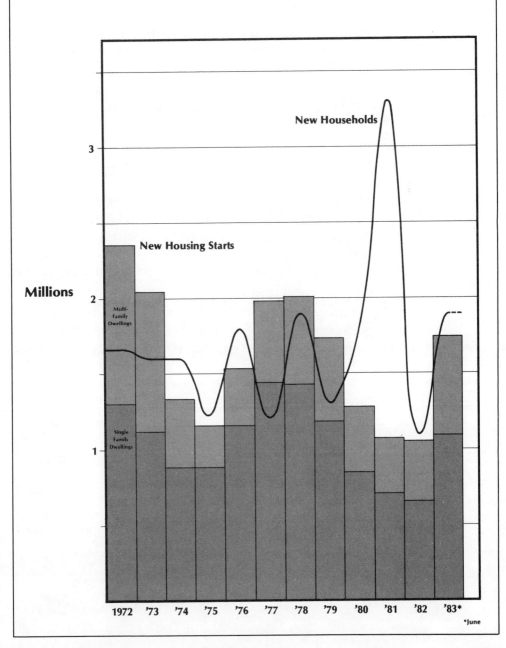

Figure 7.

Housing Demand,
1972-1983

Source: U. S. Department of Commerce

New Households

New Housing Starts

Multi-Family Dwellings

Single Family Dwellings

Millions

3

2

1

1972   '73   '74   '75   '76   '77   '78   '79   '80   '81   '82   '83*

*June

their family's home — both of which create pent-up demand and keep actual demand below projected demand. Even so, it is obvious that multifamily housing is in great demand: occupancy levels are higher than at any time since the end of World War II (see Figure 8), and the annual rate of increase in rents is also at its highest level in thirty years. Last month the annualized rate of rent increases reflected in the consumer price index (CPI) was 8.9 percent — twice the annualized inflation rate for the first quarter of 1983.

Rapidly increasing rents reflect the scarcity of new multifamily dwellings, which would offer competition to those already standing. Since it takes about one year for new multifamily dwellings to be completed, the current favorable demand/supply ratio for housing is likely to continue for at least two years.

BARRIERS TO ENTRY BY COMPETITION The reason that new multifamily dwellings are not being constructed quickly enough to keep up with the demand is that current rents do not justify current construction costs. Today, to build a garden-style apartment costs between $35 and $45 a square foot, including land and soft costs (the cost of money). In addition, because interest rates are high, holding land is expensive, and the cost of having money tied up for an extended period can add dramatically to the cost of the project.

Prospective builders are also deterred by the reluctance of lending institutions to finance multifamily housing. Lenders observe that the rents necessary to justify the cost of building a garden-style complex are between $.50 and $.60 a square foot in most parts of the country, but current rents are only $.30 to $.45 a square foot. Until rents rise 40 to 50 percent (depending on geographical area), the cost of building a new multifamily dwelling will continue to be seen as unjustifiable by lenders and builders.

TAX ADVANTAGES Over the last ten years, but particularly since the Economic Recovery Tax Act of 1981 and the Tax Equali-

Figure 8.

Vacancy Rates,
1972-1983

Source: U. S. Department of Commerce

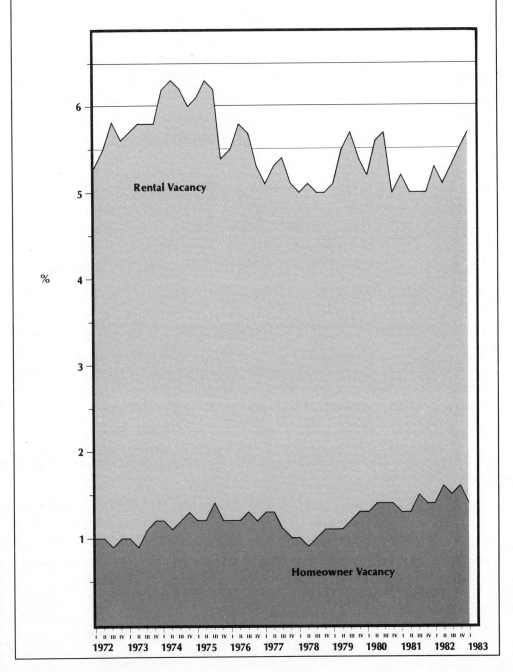

zation and Fiscal Responsibility Act of 1982, real estate has been given special tax advantages. In addition to being the only investment in which the debt remains part of the cost basis, regardless of whether there is recourse to the borrower or not, multifamily dwellings can now be depreciated over fifteen years with the 175 percent accelerated declining-balance method. This schedule enables the investor to write off enough of the investment to substantially reduce risk. For example, if an investor in the 50 percent tax bracket wrote off 100 percent of the investment, the government would in effect be subsidizing half of the investment. Only the accelerated portion of the depreciation is subject to recapture at ordinary tax rates; the balance of the depreciation would be ultimately taxable at the lower capital gains rate (maximum 20 percent). This advantageous method of taxation for housing contrasts sharply with the taxation of all other forms of depreciable real estate, for which the owner must recapture 100 percent of the depreciation at ordinary tax rates if he or she takes accelerated depreciation.

LEVERAGE   In the real estate industry, investment opportunities generally present themselves with some financing already in place. A buyer can often assume existing debt, and it is customary for the seller to carry back some paper. These practices allow a buyer to obtain additional leverage, that is, to invest with fewer at-risk dollars out of pocket. Furthermore, a motivated seller is likely to carry back paper on terms far more favorable than would be offered by a lending institution. If a seller carries back paper with no due-on-sale clause, the favorable financing automatically adds value to the property and could represent an incentive for a future buyer. In few areas of investment is practice of the seller providing credit to the buyer as widespread as in the real estate industry.

CONTROLLABILITY   With most investments one can do little to control the asset in the event of unfavorable outcomes. For example, if you buy a stock or bond and its value declines, you can only hold it or sell it. But if you invest in a multifamily dwelling and your revenues are insufficient, you have several choices. You could increase the property's value by refurbishing, landscaping, refinancing, enlarging or reducing the size of units, or changing the management style. Other options include turning the dwelling into a cooperative or a condominium. All these options involve hard work, of course, but they illustrate how the owner of a multi-family dwelling has more control over the eventual outcome of the investment than does the owner of a passive investment in which the whims of a very fickle marketplace and hundreds of uncontrollable variables can daily affect the price.

This hypothesis assumes that the owner of the apartment complex is an excellent manager, knows how best to improve the property, has a system for increasing rents, and is controlling costs — that is, that the owner is optimizing the dwelling's performance at all times. If an investor does not have the necessary expertise to manage or choose good managers, he or she may not be any better off owning an apartment investment than owning a depressed stock or bond.

SPECIAL INFORMATION

The real estate marketplace is an imperfect one; that is, the same information is not available to all participants in the market. In contrast, in a perfect marketplace, such as the ones in which stocks and bonds are traded, securities law prohibits insider information to the participants in the market. Furthermore, the stock and bond markets are true auction markets in which the prices are quoted to all parties at the same time, but the parties cannot know the true supply and demand for the commodity. In an imperfect marketplace, the true expert can obtain superior information, including an accurate knowledge of the supply and demand for the commodity. In addition, he or she can create the terms of both a sale and a purchase.

The comparative advantage afforded by special expertise is available to investors in both public and private limited partnership offerings sponsored by experts in the field of real estate. Prospective investors, however, will find it difficult to evaluate professed experts' true expertise. Any prospective investor should first investigate the sponsors of a limited partnership offering by carefully reviewing their performance record. Obviously, it is important to ascertain whether the individuals who created that record are still involved with the sponsor.

GOVERNMENT REGULATION AND INTERVENTION Government intervention in the activities of a particular industry can have a dramatic effect on the attractiveness of that industry as an investment opportunity. In this regard, the housing industry is subject to many forms of government intervention. At times, the federal government has sponsored housing projects for the needy, for low-income families, and for the aged; and government agencies have provided guarantees for conventional financing. During World War II and again in 1972, during the Nixon administration, the government imposed wage and price controls that affected rents. In addition, rent control has been imposed by state, county, and local governments in some regions.

Since housing is a necessity, it is reasonable to assume that if rents in a particular area become prohibitive, then that jurisdiction would seriously consider imposing rent control. Investors seeking to purchase apartment houses should attempt to avoid jurisdictions that seem likely to impose rent control. However, I believe that rent control will not become a widespread practice in this country because it would halt any new construction of multifamily dwellings. Further, before rents become prohibitive, I believe there will be enough incentive in the form of tax benefits for new construction to begin. Americans today are still paying on average between 25 and 30 percent of disposable income for rent, whereas in Europe and Japan rent constitutes between 40 and 50 percent of disposable income. If our spending patterns were to become more like the Europeans' and Japanese styles, the increased portion of income earmarked for rent would also encourage new construction.

Prospective investors should also note that some rent control ordinances are more prohibitive than others. For example, rent control policies in San Francisco County and Los Angeles County permit landlords enough flexibility to make property ownership still profitable. In sharp contrast, rent control in New York City is far stricter, with few increases in rent allowed, and some landlords have simply abandoned their properties because they could not make a profit. Where housing is concerned, I would prefer to invest in the sun-belt states in the South, Southwest, and Southeast, where the least local government regulation is likely.

UNIONISM

While unions have dampened the profitability of such industries as the automotive and steel industries, I don't believe that unions will substantially affect the profitability of multifamily housing ownership. It would be very difficult, almost impossible, to negotiate a union contract with a group as diverse as multifamily housing owners and multifamily housing workers. Although I can't deny that unionization is possible, I can't recall an example in which a comparable group has been unionized.

CONCLUSION

In each of the eight categories we have examined, the weight of the evidence favors multifamily housing as an investment opportunity in the next eighteen months.

Multifamily housing has not always been so attractive an investment. In 1972, the number of new housing units, including mobile homes, was approximately 1 million more than required to meet demand. Many builders lost their properties because they could not achieve the occupancy levels necessary to meet their expenses. Indeed, in the late 1960s and most of the 1970s, rents did not increase as quickly as most other components in the consumer price index because the housing industry kept pace with demand. During most of this period single-family homes for middle-income Americans were generally affordable.

Unfortunately, this trend has been reversed, and it is my conclusion that now is the best time since the end of World War II, when rents quickly doubled, to buy multifamily housing as an investment. Both private and public syndications allow individual investors to participate in this market if they do not have the capital and expertise to do so on their own. Recall that in the 1970s those who invested with adequate reserves in carefully selected and well-managed real estate generally did well. And if the results were good during a decade of overbuilding, they should be even better now that housing is relatively unaffordable and few new multifamily dwellings are being built. Current prices, though historically high, may well seem bargains within twenty-four months, and those who invest in the right multifamily opportunities will be very gratified indeed.

Chapter
Six

The Great
Equity Lock-In

Real estate has, of course, not always been the glamorous investment it is today. During the 1950s and 1960s it generally appreciated commensurate with inflation, about 2.5 percent in the 1950s and 3.5 percent in the 1960s. This was not nearly as lucrative as the stock market which outpaced inflation by a wide margin.

But as you've just learned in Chapter 5, real estate became the investment of choice in the 1970s, often growing at double the 7 percent inflation rate. And if your investment was leveraged at three dollars of debt to a dollar of equity (you borrowed three dollars to put into the property for every dollar invested of your own money) results were astounding. Assuming the property had a compounded appreciation rate of 15 percent, your money would have increased at a 28 percent compounded annual rate. That means for every dollar you invested in the holding, your return was $2.80 per annum. Your equity was doubling every 2.6 years. If you bought a home in 1970 at $20,000, with a $15,000 mortgage, by the end of the decade the property was probably worth over $80,000. Your equity grew during this period to between $65,000 and $70,000.

The same was not true for owners of office buildings, shopping centers and apartment complexes. For them appreciation depended more on rent increases than on replacement cost, the main factor affecting the value of homes. Since home replacement costs rose much faster in the 1970s than rents, homes appreciated much faster than most income-producing real estate.

Despite this difference, both home owners and owners of income producing real estate faced a common problem — freeing up their locked-in equity. This was the result of a problem that developed during the last half of the 1970s. Lenders resisted making long-term loans at fixed interest rates. After the 1973–75 recession, fixed interest rate mortgages were replaced by a flood of new products that were a great deal for the bankers. Some had ominous sounding names, like bullet loans with a three to five year payoff period. Variable rate mortgages permitted rates to rise as frequently as twice a year. There was a negative amortization mortgage, where part of the interest was paid currently and part accrued to a balloon payment. Equally unattractive was the shared equity mortgage where the lender became a co-owner. Who wants a bank as a joint tenant?

Since these new loans seemed unattractive, many property owners simply left their equity locked in their property or arranged a short-term commercial loan and assigned their property as collateral. But this was only a temporary solution to the locked-in equity problem, because the bank making the commercial loan would insist that the loan be paid back within twelve months and would give no assurances that the loan could be renewed. There are, however, several ways to unlock the equity from real property without the owner taking on the burden of unattractive financing.

JOINT VENTURES The joint venture is an excellent tool for pulling equity out of a property without taking on new debt and, in many cases, without even paying any income tax as a result of a property transfer. If a property owner with locked equity contributes the property to a joint venture partnership and a joint venture partner contributes cash, the real property contributor may, in many instances, pull out cash from the joint venture partnership as a withdrawal of capital without triggering a taxable event. Such agreements, however, are affected by many nuances of the tax laws, and a property owner should consult with a professional tax advisor before

72

entering into such an arrangement. The two main factors to be considered in arranging the partnership are (1) to ensure that a large tax consequence does not follow from the debt on the property being larger than the basis, and (2) to ensure that the capital to be pulled out after the joint venture is formed has resided in the joint venture for a sufficient period of time.

This technique enables the owner of a property to continue owning a large percentage of the property and still free up his or her equity for diversified investments in other real property or other kinds of assets. Two inducements for the cash-contributing partner are that he or she would receive a priority cash flow on the investment and a priority return of capital. In such a case, the joint venture partner would resemble a preferred stockholder, and the contributor of the property would resemble a common stockholder.

SYNDICATION

Syndicating income property is essentially a sale, but it gives the owner the added advantage of retaining a promoter's interest or a general partner's interest while, at the same time, freeing most of his or her equity. If the owner does not know how to syndicate the property, he or she can work with a professional syndicator. While this approach will increase the property owner's costs in the transaction, the additional expenses can easily be offset either by the syndicator's ability to obtain a better price for the property or by the owner's receiving a promoter's interest in the property.

SELLING THE PROPERTY OUTRIGHT

If an owner does not mind selling the property, an easy solution to the locked-in equity problem is to sell, pull out as much equity as possible, pay the taxes, and carry back as much paper as necessary to facilitate the sale. However, many owners who have chosen this option find that a great deal of their equity is still locked up in the paper they carry back. Furthermore, the sale carries substantial tax disadvantages.

Such sellers might well have done better with either a joint venture or a syndication in which they maintained a promoter's interest in the property. For many, borrowing from a three-year lender with equity kickers (lender's equity participation) and high interest rates is a better option than selling the property, since most sellers take accelerated depreciation and have quite a tax burden at the time of the sale. Under the current tax regulations, a seller has to recapture all accelerated depreciation as ordinary income, then pay capital gains tax on the difference between his cost basis and the sales price. In addition, if his mortgage exceeds his basis, he must pay tax on that difference in the year of sale. The seller cannot avoid the capital gains tax, since the IRS will charge a maximum of 20 percent on the excluded portion of the capital gain as an alternative minimum tax. Thus sellers who can pull their equity out of a property without selling will realize considerable savings in taxes.

NATIONAL BENEFITS OF THE GREAT EQUITY LOCK-IN

The 1970s created enormous hidden wealth for Americans in the form of locked-in equity in their real property. For most owners, it simply makes good sense to unlock the equity and either diversify their assets or buy more real estate. Whether an owner of property decides to syndicate, sell, or pull out equity through financing, part of the proceeds inevitably will be used to help fund other business opportunities and new construction. Thus as property owners become more liquid, the nation's economic recovery will be enhanced.

Many owners can be expected to reinvest their funds in new construction or new business opportunities, and it is fair to assume that such activity will stimulate the economy as a whole. Estimates of the growth in real estate equities in this country during the 1970s run over $1 trillion. If only 20 percent of that equity were to be released and then used in either new business ventures or new real estate development over the next five years, the gross national product (GNP) would be enhanced dramatically, both from the velocity of money changing hands and from the resulting additional employment opportunities.

The liquidation of some of this enormous untapped equity will also constitute a new market for banks and savings and loans should depository savings continue to increase in this nation. Without question, the great real estate wealth that exists in this country will ultimately be the collateral for many of the financings that will further stimulate the nation's economy in the 1980s.

Anthony Downs of the Brookings Institute recently summarized the performance of real estate in relation to inflation: "The net return to ownership of real estate in absolute dollars tends to vary about in proportion to the rate of inflation, even if that rate has not been forecast in advance. It provides a means of coping with the inherent impossibility of predicting future inflation rates accurately." CONCLUSION

Since ownership of real estate, whether it be a home or income-producing property, tends to increase as inflation increases, the inflationary trend in the economy should produce more owners who accumulate enormous equity, and they can be expected to look for opportunities to free up that equity to reinvest in other areas.

Those who trade in real estate should do very well indeed in the next ten years because the inflationary trend will probably continue to benefit real estate owners more than at any time in history. Too, real estate is in short supply compared to the likely future demand, and it is the one product that cannot be imported at a cheaper price.

Chapter
Seven

Hypothecation
Loans

In the 1950s, 1960s and early 1970s, mortgage rates were relatively stable, fluctuating less than ten percent a year. Buildings were bought and sold with financing from banks, savings and loans or mortgage companies. But since 1975, outside mortgage financing has been prohibitively expensive. Banks cut themselves out of many deals by asking for as much as 18 percent interest. This forced sellers to become their own bankers, carrying loans personally. This "creative financing" meant that sellers would charge a relatively low interest rate on the note in exchange for a higher purchase price.

Few sellers were willing to carry back paper for longer than ten years, and at least half specified periods shorter than a decade. This arrangement put buyers in jeopardy when they were unable to pay off or refinance balloon payments required when the mortgage came due. Sellers, with little or no inclination to foreclose on the building, in turn found themselves in jeopardy with these "problem loans." The sellers could either extend the term of the loan or sell paper at a discount to a third party. Unfortunately this becomes, in effect, a forced sale, where the seller unloads the mortgage for less than its true value. Typically a discounted sale of the loan could wipe out a third of the seller's profit. Even worse, the sale of this paper was taxed as a capital gain. Thus "creative financing" became a euphemism for sellers taking a beating in the real estate market.

Is there a way out of this self-defeating syndrome? I believe there is a promising alternative that will be used extensively during this decade to help real estate sellers earn the maximum profit. It's called a hypothecation loan.

Let's assume you sell a property worth $1 million with a $400,000 first mortgage. You carry back $300,000 in a second deed of trust payable in seven years, interest only at 10 percent. The annual payment due you on the loan is $30,000. In this example, you should be able to borrow at least half of the $300,000 second deed, or $150,000, by making an absolute assignment of the note to a bank. This is an extremely secure loan from the bank's point of view. If you do not repay the bank, the bank is in the same position you are in the note: able to foreclose on a property whose debt-to-value ratio is only 70 percent. Furthermore, assuming you pay the bank 15 percent on the hypothecation loan, the bank's debt coverage is excellent — roughly 1.3 to 1 — because you're collecting $30,000 and paying out to the bank only $22,500. Most banks will not want to make such a loan at a fixed rate; they would rather have a rate that moves up or down with the prime rate or some other index. But all banks are likely to negotiate a floor and a ceiling rate, say, 12 and 18 percent.

Banks are going to become increasingly interested in hypothecation loans because the recession and the new tax laws that provide incentives for personal saving have created an unusual set of circumstances. The recession has caused many borrowers to be unable to pay off their current debts, and therefore they are not seeking new loans. At the same time, the rate of saving has been stimulated by such vehicles as individual retirement accounts (IRAs), all-savers accounts, money market rate accounts, and six-month Treasury bill certificate of deposit accounts. Between mid 1980 and mid 1983, savings jumped from 4.5 percent to over 7 percent of personal income. Thus banks find themselves with fewer credit-worthy borrowers and high deposits.

Now, banks find very attractive a loan with $2 equity for every $1 of debt ($300,000 equity in the note against $150,000 borrowed) and 4 to 1 debt protection if the bank forecloses ($300,000 equity in the loan plus $300,000 equity in the building against $150,000 loaned). In addition to this collateral, a banker will insist that the borrower also sign personally for the loan; if all else fails, the banker retains the usual recourse for collection of personal loans. The following example illustrates how bankers should look at this loan:

Bank's Security

Value of property securing debt	$1,000,000
Second note and deed of trust	300,000
First note and deed of trust	400,000
Equity in property	300,000
	$1,000,000

Collateral to Bank

Second note	300,000
Equity on property	300,000
	$ 600,000
Equity coverage	600,000 ÷ 150,000 = 4 to 1

Debt Coverage Ratio

Debt payment coverage:	
payment on second note	30,000
Payment to bank at average rate	
of 15 percent	22,500
Debt coverage ratio	30,000 ÷ 22,500 = 1.33 to 1

For the seller who is carrying the second deed, a hypothecation loan has more-favorable tax consequences than either refinancing the debt or selling the note at discount. Whereas the latter two would involve taxable capital gains, a hypothecation loan is simply the

TAX ADVANTAGES

use of a debt instrument as collateral for a loan and does not constitute a taxable event. Furthermore, a hypothecation loan allows the seller to continue to defer any taxable gains until the balloon payment comes due on the note. Thus the seller can rationalize paying a higher interest rate than usual on a refinancing transaction. In addition, by taking out a hypothecation loan rather than selling the note at discount, the holder of the note will receive the full $300,000 balloon payment when it comes due, or $150,000 after paying off the bank the hypothecation loan, rather than having to give a 35 to 40 percent discount on the note.

PACKAGING LOANS FOR HYPOTHECATION

I have seen firsthand the packaging and hypothecation of $12 million worth of wraparound mortgage loans, some in a second position and others in a third position to the mortgages already on the properties, to a bank that was willing to loan half the equity in the notes. This transaction completely cashed out more than 2,000 investors from a large public real estate syndication sponsored by the company with which I'm associated. The investors were absolutely delighted because both their tax advantages and their profits remained intact. This transaction was not a bit difficult for the bank, which was used to factoring paper for several large retail clients, and the banker was pleased because he perceived that the bank had far more security in the real estate transaction than in many other loans it was carrying. Let me add that this loan was made by a bank that had not done any business with our company prior to this hypothecation loan.

HYPOTHECATION LOANS IMPROVE THE INTERNAL RATE OF RETURN

In the partnership mentioned above, the after-tax internal rate of return (IRR) to the investor jumped from approximately 16 percent to approximately 18 percent even though the interest rate on the hypothecation loan was higher than the rate earned on the notes collateralizing the loan. This will almost always be the case because IRR is a function of not merely the overall flow of income but also the flow of income in the earlier years. Because the partners cashed out of the partnership three years earlier than if they had waited for balloon payments on the wraparound notes, and since taxable gains were deferred for three years, the net result was that the investors realized a superior IRR. Further, and most important, the investors had the use of $6 million three years earlier to invest in another opportunity.

In making a hypothecation loan, a bank need not evaluate the properties as carefully as it would for refinancing because the amount of exposure is not as great. The note-holder is not asking the banker to refinance the property, which would require a formal appraisal on the property and a vigorous evaluation: indeed, some banks are at times reluctant to make any real estate loans.

HYPOTHECATION LOANS CAN BE MORE EXPEDITIOUS THAN REFINANCING

In contrast, a hypothecation loan for only half the equity in the paper to be assigned more closely resembles a commercial loan transaction, and the banker can be satisfied by a more cursory evaluation of the property securing the note. Since the bank will be looking to the note-holder for personal recourse in the event the homeowner defaults on the note, the credibility of the note-holder is just as important as, if not more important than, the value of the property. Therefore, a banker will often respond much more quickly to a hypothecation loan than to a refinancing of the loan.

Hypothecation loans will become prevalent in the 1980s because they make sense from both the note-holder's and the bank's point of view. They will also become popular because in the last seven years an enormous amount of paper has been created by sellers to facilitate real estate transactions. Holders of that paper will be looking for the best way to turn that paper into cash.

CONCLUSION

As we have seen, hypothecation loans are attractive to banks because of their security (debt coverage) and resemblances to personal and commercial loans. The loans are attractive to note-holders because of their favorable tax consequences and overall profitability.

Note-holders, however, should observe two cautions when arranging a hypothecation loan: first, the loan should have a ceiling interest rate; second, the term of the loan should be at least as long as the note being hypothecated, and preferably six months longer, if that can be arranged. This second precaution will protect the note-holder in case the hypothecated note is not paid off on time. By following these cautions and pursuing hypothecation loans as part of the total real estate transaction, an investor should significantly increase his or her internal rate of return on investment.

*Chapter
Eight*

*Leveraged
Real Estate
in Tax Exempt
Qualified Plans*

One of the primary reasons people buy real estate is for its tax advantages. While appreciation potential is important, many investors also pay for the substantial value of depreciation. Surprisingly, most managers of retirement funds and investors who have set up a tax-exempt qualified plan ignore leveraged real estate. That's because they know that income or capital gains from leveraged real estate could generate what the IRS calls "unrelated business income" subject to taxation. Since the whole point of a tax-exempt qualified plan is to avoid taxes, they prefer not to get involved. Indeed, on the surface, any taxation looks like a mistake for a qualified plan dedicated to deferring taxable income. But in many cases the benefits outweigh the burdens. Here's why qualified plans should consider leveraged real estate investments.

Let's look at the tax liability of a qualified plan that sells leveraged real estate. The IRS says the plan has to pay capital gains tax on that portion of the gain equaling the proportion of highest debt (twelve months prior to the date of sale) to the property's average tax basis in the year of sale. For example if a tax-exempt entity buys a property for $1 million cash and later sells it for $1.2 million no taxes are due. That's because there was no debt in the original all cash deal. But what happens when the same qualified plan decides to buy the identical property with a down payment of $250,000 and takes out a $750,000 mortgage? When the property is sold for $1.2 million, the IRS multiplies the $200,000 profit by 75 percent. But then it allows a profit-sharing or pension trust a 60 percent exclusion on the leveraged portion of the gain. (This tax is calculated under the income tax

POTENTIAL TAX LIABILITY OF LEVERAGED REAL ESTATE

tables for estates and trusts under Section 1(e) of the Internal Revenue Code.)

If the taxpayer elects to treat the sale on the installment-sale basis, the tax to be paid for the year of sale would be based on the payments made during that year and not on the entire gain realized. Currently, it is unclear whether any payments received beyond the year of sale would be taxable since the asset is no longer leveraged real estate but, instead, a note receivable. In any case, even if installments received subsequent to the year of sale were subject to tax, the tax would normally be less than that payable if the entire gain were taxed in the year of sale.

SAMPLE TRANSACTIONS

Let us assume that a qualified plan realizes a $33,330 capital gain (payable equally over five years), and the debt-to-basis ratio was 75 percent. The taxable portion of the gain — $25,000 (75% × $33,330) — would be spread equally over five years; thus only $2,000 (40% × $5,000) would be taxable in each of those years. But there is also a specific exemption of $1,000 a year on unrelated business income. So in this example, the trust would pay taxes on the remaining $1,000 a year of unrelated business income. If this were the only unrelated business income in the qualified plan, the tax rate would be 14 percent, the lowest current rate. The tax in this case would be $140 in each of the five years, for a total tax of $700 against a profit of $25,000. Moreover, this tax could be further reduced if the trust had a net operating loss carried forward as a result of "shelter" generated from the investment in prior years.

The following calculations summarize this example:

Capital gain (installment-sale basis)	$33,330
Capital gain related to debt-to-basis ratio (75% × $33,330)	25,000

Annual taxable income (spread equally over five years)		5,000
Taxable income after exclusion (40% × $5,000)		2,000
Specific $1,000 yearly exemption	(	1,000)
Net taxable income to trust		1,000
Tax due each year		140
Total taxes over five years		700
Total taxes as a percentage of $33,330 capital gain		2.1%

Moreover, if we use the same example but have the trust realize the entire profit in one year, its tax liability would be $1,800 (before the application of any net operating loss carry forward):

Capital gain		$33,330
Capital gain related to debt-to-basis ratio (75% × $33,330)		25,000
Taxable income after exclusion (40% × $25,000)		10,000
Specific $1,000 yearly exemption	(	1,000)
Net taxable		9,000
Total tax due (rounded)		1,800
Total tax as a percentage of $33,330 capital gain		5.4%

OTHER SHELTER

Depreciation from income-producing real estate can shelter the rental income normally taxable to the trust in the same proportion as average debt to the average tax basis of the property. This would certainly be the case with an apartment complex in which the leverage is at least $3 of debt to $1 of equity. Naturally, the amount of yearly depreciation would depend on the number of years over which the improvement was to be depreciated, and it would also depend on the ratio of land value to improvement value. Obviously, the larger the value of the improvement (in proportion to the value of the land), the greater the likelihood that all the income would be sheltered. It should be noted, however, that only straight-line depreciation may be used to compute taxable income with respect to leveraged real estate in a profit-sharing or pension plan.

TO LEVERAGE OR NOT
TO LEVERAGE? As we have seen, leveraged real estate can generate a tax liability for a qualified plan, but the liability, particularly after being mitigated by depreciation and exemptions, will often represent only a very small percentage of the total income generated. Thus leveraged real estate is an option for qualified plans, and in many cases it will result in better overall rates of return than other investments in the portfolio despite potential tax liabilities. This is not to say that all retirement plans should be leaping into leveraged real estate. Quite the opposite. The decision is a thorny one that should be approached cautiously.

The decision to purchase leveraged investments for a profit-sharing or pension plan should be considered when the potential reward seems well worth the burden. The most common investments found in pension and profit-sharing trusts are stock and bonds. Unfortunately, the maximum leverage on bonds is 70 percent; on stocks, it's 50 percent. Typically, leverage on stocks and bonds is at a floating rate of 1 to 2 points over prime, and the loans are callable. In contrast, income-producing real estate quite commonly is leveraged between 70 to 80 percent for twenty-five to thirty years at a fixed interest rate. In inflationary times, the leverage advantage is highly likely to offset the possible tax burdens associated with unrelated business income.

The one problem that leveraged real estate cannot avoid is illiquidity. Stocks and bonds are instantly liquid. To the extent that instant liquidity may be needed, a tax-exempt entity should not invest in real estate or even limited partnership interests in real estate. But consider that most pension and profit-sharing plans have a mixture of employees who will be retiring at various times. As long as the proportion of liquid assets to illiquid assets is sufficient to take care of those who are going to be retiring within a relatively short period of time, there should be no problem with having a prudent percentage of the total trust portfolio in leveraged real estate (whether outright ownership or a limited partnership interest).

[The following summary has been prepared by Bronson, Bronson & McKinnon, special tax counsel to the Consolidated Capital Companies.] SOME CAVEATS

Status of Plan as a Dealer. If a qualified plan were treated as a "dealer" with respect to real property, all the gain from the sale of such property (not just the leveraged portion) would be subject to federal income tax. In addition, the 60 percent exclusion for long-term capital gains would be unavailable, and, therefore, the entire gain would be taxed at ordinary income tax rates. The plan would be treated as a dealer if it held the property primarily for sale to customers in the ordinary course of its trade or business. Whether a taxpayer is a dealer is a mixed question of law and fact and needs to be considered on an individual case basis.

New Legislation. The section of the Internal Revenue Code of 1954 that sets forth the provisions on leveraged investments and qualified plans was amended during December 1980. Effective for taxable years of a plan beginning after 31 December 1980, the amendment provides that, with five exceptions, debt incurred by a plan with respect to real estate investments will not cause a qualified plan to generate unrelated business income.

The exceptions referred to above provide that if the debt is incurred in connection with any one of the following circumstances, the real estate will generate unrelated business income:

1. The purchase price of the real property is not a fixed amount determined as of the date of acquisition.

2. The amount of indebtedness, the purchase price,

or the amount of timing of any payment are dependent, in whole or in part, upon future revenues, income, or profits derived from the property.

3. The real property is leased back to the seller, or to a "related person."

4. The real property is acquired from, or is at any time after the acquisition leased by a qualified plan to, certain "disqualified persons."

5. The debt is a nonrecourse debt owed to the transferor of the property, a "related person" to the transferor, or a "disqualified person," which debt either is subordinate to any other indebtedness secured by the property or bears a rate of interest significantly less than that which would apply if financing had been obtained from an independent third party.

The code provides detailed definitions of the terms *related person* and *disqualified person*. Complex ownership attribution rules apply.

Valuation. An investment in real estate by a qualified plan, either directly or indirectly through the purchase of a limited partnership interest, may present a valuation problem for the plan administrator. Normally, the assets of a plan are valued annually for a number of purposes. In the case of a defined contribution plan (e.g., profit-sharing plan), the valuation is necessary in order to determine the extent of each participant's interest in the plan. Since there may not be a ready market for the real estate or the interest in the partnership, it may be difficult to obtain an accurate valuation. Nonetheless, this is only one factor that should be considered, and the difficulty (but not impossibility) of valuation may be outweighed by the advantages of such an investment.

Prohibited Transactions. Section 4975 of the Internal Revenue Code prohibits certain transactions between a "disqualified party" and a qualified plan. The code sets forth a detailed list of those persons who would constitute disqualified parties, which would include participants in the plan and the sponsoring employer. With certain exceptions, the purchase and sale or leasing of property, or the loan of funds between such disqualified persons and the plan is prohibited. See also sections 406 through 408 of the Employee Retirement Income Security Act of 1974 (ERISA). Other transactions are also prohibited, but those mentioned above are among the ones most common in real estate transactions. All such transactions should be carefully reviewed.

Plan Assets. ERISA imposes certain obligations on fiduciaries with respect to the investment of the assets of an employee benefit plan. For example, section 404 of ERISA requires fiduciaries to invest plan assets "with the care, skill, prudence, and diligence under the circumstances then prevailing that a prudent man acting in a like capacity and familiar with such matters would use in the conduct of an enterprise of a like character and with like aims" and to diversify "the investments of a plan so as to minimize the risk of large losses, unless under the circumstances it is clearly prudent not to do so." Obviously, such considerations, among others, must be taken into account by fiduciaries in investing plan assets.

The Department of Labor recently proposed regulations defining the term *plan assets*. These regulations could have applications for investments in a limited partnership and, in some cases, in a corporation. One usually thinks of a plan's assets as consisting of the shares of stock in the case of a corporation or a limited partnership interest in the case of a partnership. The proposed regulations, however, provide that under certain circumstances, the assets of a plan include the plan's share of the underlying assets of the corporation or the partnership. If this were the case, the general partners of the partnership may be deemed to be fiduciaries of the plan and, therefore, would be subject to all the restrictions and limitations applicable to fiduciaries.

Summary. Each pension and profit-sharing plan has its own idiosyncracies, and investments should be made on the basis of each particular plan's objectives, the timing of beneficiary retirements, and, of course, the available investment expertise. If expertise for investing in income-producing real estate is available, then the unrelated business income tax should not (in itself) be a prohibiting factor.

Chapter Nine

Tax Planning with Real Estate Partnerships

Clifford Trusts, irrevocable trusts and the Uniform Gifts to Minors Act are not exactly the stuff of cocktail party talk. Although these subjects are primarily the domain of tax lawyers and accountants, they make a difference to anyone who joins a real estate limited partnership. These three methods are ideal tax-planning tools for high-income earners who want to pass income to members in their family who are in lower tax brackets. And by using them in conjunction with real estate limited partnerships, you can enjoy significant tax savings which may not be possible with alternative investments.

All three of these devices can help move income out of the 50 percent maximum individual income tax rate to lower rates. They also can take advantage of gift tax exclusions. As you'll see from the following examples, this is not the do-it-yourself arena of estate planning. Complicated tax rules and accounting procedures make expert advice mandatory. I've been in this business for 20 years and wouldn't consider tax planning without the aid of accounting experts. For as we speak a judge somewhere in this great land of ours is reinterpreting the federal tax code.

Clifford trusts are an ideal tax-planning tool for high-income earners who want to build up an education fund for their young children. The use of real estate limited partnerships to fund such a vehicle can, at the same time, provide considerable tax savings. **CLIFFORD TRUSTS**

A Clifford trust combines characteristics of an irrevocable trust with characteristics of a revocable trust: it cannot be revoked for ten years, but at the end of this period the assets of the trust may revert back to the donor. Consequently, no federal gift tax is payable, since the owner always has a reversionary interest.[1] But for the first ten years, all the ordinary income from the trust is vested in the beneficiary and is taxed at the beneficiary's tax bracket.

While a conventional Clifford trust does not serve to redirect capital gains income into the beneficiary's tax bracket, it may be possible to design a Clifford trust under which capital gains and the recapture of accelerated depreciation from real estate limited partnerships would be taxed in the beneficiary's tax bracket. Further, under this plan the donor might completely avoid the imposition of an alternative minimum tax, which might be triggered were the capital gain attributed to the donor, by designating in the trust instrument that all gains from the sale of capital assets accrue to trust income rather than to trust principal.

Three cautionary notes should be sounded in this regard. First, such a clause may serve to increase the extent to which the transfer exhausts the taxpayer's unified transfer credit, with the possibility that the Internal Revenue Service would contend that the taxpayer's credit should be reduced by the full amount of the trust principal in excess of $10,000 per donor per donee.[2] Second, if capital assets were sold by a trust within two years of their receipt by that trust, then gain attributable to unrealized appreciation that preceded the transfer into trust is taxed in the donor's bracket rather than in that of the beneficiary. Third, due regard should be given to applicable state law in the drafting of any such provision. After ten years have elapsed, the remaining assets of the trust would revert back to the donor, so that he or she would retain ultimate control of the trust's assets.

Let us consider an example. A married couple filing a joint return has $60,000 net taxable earned income and owns an interest in a real estate limited partnership from which they know they have a potential long-term capital gain of $20,000 (of which the $8,000 subject to tax would be taxed at a 49 percent marginal rate, for a total tax liability of $3,920[3]). In addition, they have sufficient other net capital gains and other items of tax preference such that they would be liable for a 20 percent alternative minimum tax on the $12,000 excluded portion of the potential $20,000 capital gain.

This couple is considering establishing a Clifford trust with their child as the beneficiary. If the child has no outside income, the income tax payable by the child on the long-term capital gain would be only $791, and there would be no alternative minimum tax liability:

	Capital Gains Tax	Alternative Minimum Tax	Total Taxes
Parents' tax	$3,920	$80	$4,000
Child's tax			
(using Clifford trust):	791	-0-	791

The couple would thus realize a tax savings of $3,209. This strategy is entirely within the boundaries of sound tax planning and does not preclude the donor from future use of the remaining assets, as they revert back to the donor at the end of ten years.

IRREVOCABLE TRUSTS

The Tax Reform Act of 1976 made the gift tax and the estate tax identical and unified. For federal tax purposes, gifts made after 1976 are added back into the estate at the donor's death, and then a credit is given for the gift taxes already paid. The unification of the gift tax and estate tax has prompted individuals concerned with the estate tax to consider making their gifts before the asset has actually appreciated. This strategy excludes from the donor's estate *both* the value of the asset on the date of the gift *and* all appreciation that takes place after the gift is made. These sums, therefore, will not be subject to estate taxes, and any gift taxes paid will reduce the taxpayer's ultimate taxable estate. The donor, however, does lose the use of any money paid as gift taxes.

For example, let's look at the case of an unmarried individual who used up his unified credit through gifts and still leaves a $500,000 net taxable estate. Suppose he had set up an irrevocable trust to which he had donated $10,000 in the form of real estate limited partnership units. Subsequent to the gift, the units appreciated enough to create a $20,000 capital gain. Without the trust, the $500,000 estate would be taxed $155,800 — since the unified credit was exhausted — and any additional assets over $500,000 and up to $750,000 would be taxed at 37 percent.

With the trust, the estate would save $7,400 (37% × $20,000) because the appreciation on the real estate would not be subject to federal estate tax on the death of the donor. Since most states (but not California) have inheritance taxes, additional tax savings would accrue, depending on the donor's state of residence at the time of death. No federal gift tax liability would be generated by the $10,000 since the gift would be subject to the $10,000 annual exclusion (assuming that the annual exclusion had not otherwise been used). To summarize:

	Estate	Tax
Donor (assuming gift not made)	$520,000	$163,200
Donor (having made gift)	500,000	155,800
Federal estate tax savings		7,400
Federal gift tax liability		-0-
Federal tax savings (estate and gift)		$ 7,400

Methods that have been used in the past, and which may be used in the future, for determining value at the time a nonliquid real estate limited partnership unit is assigned as a gift include the following:

- most recent sale of the unit
- appraised value of the unit, if available
- original cost of the unit
- original cost of the unit, less depreciation
- liquidation value

The Internal Revenue Service may or may not find any one of these methods exclusively satisfactory and may wish to use a combination of them to determine value. Should the IRS undervalue the unit, one may realize a savings in the amount of the assessed gift tax.

In order to achieve all the tax benefits discussed here, a gift must be complete, must not be used to benefit the donor, and must be a gift of a present rather than a future interest. Thus, for example, if the donor retains any reversionary interest, right of revocation or modification, or power of appointment that will give him or her the option to change beneficiaries at will, the gift is not completed and the assets remain taxable in the donor's estate.

In addition, the donor cannot in any way use the gift to his or her own advantage after it is made. For example, neither the income nor the principal of a trust may be used to discharge the expenses of a child beneficiary that fall within the donor-parent's state law support obligations. To the extent that such income is used to benefit the donor, it will be taxed to him or her.

Finally, as a general rule, the trust instrument should mandate the distribution of all trust income to the beneficiary and not allow it to be accumulated in the trust. If the trustee is permitted to accumulate income, the transfer into trust will generally be considered that of a future interest and will not be available for the $10,000 per donee, per donor annual exclusion.[4]

One of the best ways to avoid both the estate tax and gift tax is to take advantage of the annual $10,000 gift tax exclusion. This exclusion allows an individual taxpayer to give $10,000 each to an unlimited number of individuals each year without any gift tax or future estate tax ramifications. In addition, a married couple in both community property and non—community property states can give a total of $20,000 to each of an unlimited number of individuals each year without any gift tax or future estate tax ramifications.

ANNUAL $10,000 GIFT TAX EXCLUSION

One of the simplest ways to give a gift to minor children is to donate the gift under the Uniform Gifts to Minors Act. By using the provisions of this act, one avoids the legal expenses and trouble of setting up a special trust. The child will automatically become the outright owner of the asset when he or she reaches the age of majority, as defined by applicable state law.

A gift of real estate limited partnership units may give the child several advantages unavailable through other investment alternatives. For example, the gift may produce capital gains in addition to ordinary income, and the child may benefit from the installment method of reporting gains on sales. Also, benefits from the real estate program may be realized over a period of time (assuming notes are carried back on the sale of the real estate assets), as opposed to the child's receiving the entire proceeds of the assets in one lump sum, an amount that might create more burden than benefit. Finally, the child may develop an early appreciation for real estate as an investment medium, which may be valuable to his or her future.

One cautionary note regarding the use of this vehicle: the donor should appoint someone other than himself or herself to be the custodian of a gift under the Uniform Gifts to Minors Act. Failure to do so may cause the amount of the gift to remain in the donor's gross estate for estate tax purposes.

THE LARGER THE ESTATE, THE LARGER THE TAX CONSEQUENCES

Because gift and estate taxes are progressive, gift giving in estate planning becomes increasingly important for larger estates. For example, for gifts made in 1983 and decedents dying in 1983, the gift or estate tax after using the unified credit and expressed as a percentage of the net taxable estate is: up to $275,000 — 0 percent; $500,000 — 15.3 percent; $1 million — 26.7 percent; and $3.5 million — 43 percent.[5] Estate assets over $3.5 million are taxed at a rate of 65 percent. Note, furthermore, that other tax credits are available, including a credit for state inheritance taxes.

If the annual rate of inflation in the next two or three decades approaches 6 to 7 percent, almost every American now earning a middle income will eventually face an estate tax problem. Consider the following: A large number of married couples now earn a combined annual income of $25,000. Their salaries can be expected to increase with the cost of living such that within ten years their income could be approximately $50,000, even if they were not to receive merit increases or promotions. At the end of another ten or twelve years their income can be expected to double again, to approximately $100,000. THE EFFECT OF INFLATION ON FUTURE ESTATES

As these estimates indicate, it may not be uncommon in the future for a middle-income American family to accumulate a lifetime estate in excess of the amount exempt from federal gift and estate taxes. A middle-income family in the future may very well average $40,000 to $50,000 a year, earning between $1 million and $2 million over a forty-year period. Upper middle-income Americans may earn between $2.5 million and $3 million in their forty-year work span. Obviously, such income and its potential tax ramifications — both in terms of annual income tax, as well as the future gift and estate taxes — demand the attention of well-trained financial planners and the expert counsel of certified public accountants and attorneys specializing in taxation.

Any individual who is considering any one of the tax-planning strategies discussed in this chapter should consult with a tax expert or a financial planning counselor. A thorough analysis of both the nuances of the tax laws and the particulars of an individual's complete financial situation are necessary to successful tax planning — and such analysis can be made only by expert counselors. TAX PLANNING REQUIRES EXPERT ASSISTANCE

Thus no individual should attempt to act on any of the general strategies in this chapter without adequate professional counsel.[6]

[1] If the trust contains a provision that allows the reversion to pass to someone other than the donor if he or she is not alive on the date of the termination of the trust, some states (but not California) would impose a state gift tax payable on the reversion.

[2] Or, if the unified credit had already been exhausted, such a clause could serve appreciably to increase the gift tax liability of the donor. Each investor will have to determine whether, under his or her particular circumstances, the tax benefits of such a clause would outweigh the potential adverse transfer-tax consequences.

[3] All tax liabilities are computed using rates applicable to the taxable year ending 31 December 1983, as established by the Economic Recovery Tax Act of 1981.

[4] An important exception to this general rule permits the custodian of a gift made to a minor under the Uniform Gifts to Minors Act to accumulate income up until the date on which the beneficiary reaches majority, at which time all accumulated income together with the asset are to be transferred to the beneficiary. The term *minor* is defined by the applicable state law; current definitions range between 18 and 21 years of age. (See the discussion of this act later in this chapter.) As an alternative to making a gift under the Uniform Gifts to Minors Act, it is possible for a trust to accumulate income prior to and past the age at which the beneficiary reaches majority if the trust contains a Crummey power. This technique should be discussed with a tax attorney.

[5] The unified credit in 1983 is equivalent to a taxable estate of $275,000, and the maximum federal estate and gift tax marginal rate is 65 percent. The unified credit is to increase each year so that after 1986, $600,000 may pass free of federal estate and gift tax. Moreover, the maximum gift and estate tax rate is to decline such that after 1984 the maximum marginal rate is 50 percent.

[6] Bronson, Bronson & McKinnon, of San Francisco, California, as special tax and corporate counsel to Consolidated Capital Companies, has reviewed and approved the foregoing material for purposes of application of the applicable federal tax laws under the Economic Recovery Tax Act of 1981 (ERTA).

Part
Three

Techniques for
Evaluating

Investments —
and Increasing
Profits

Chapter
Ten

Creative
Financing

What is "creative financing"? It refers simply to alternatives to traditional mortgage financing. When money is tight unreasonable interest rates make it difficult to arrange mortgage loans through banks or savings and loans. That's why many buyers and sellers turn to creative financing. When funds are easily available from lending institutions, even better creative financing options are often available.

How hard is it to use creative financing? Not very, if you learn some straightforward techniques to identify the true costs and benefits of this approach. If you want to approach real estate deals like a savvy expert, learn these relatively simple methods. Inevitably they lead to better deals. Using these techniques you can calculate the relative value of fixed vs. variable-rate financing. You can find ways to convince sellers who want all cash to carry back paper. And there are several methods that help both parties from a tax standpoint. What comes across in many of these deals is the fact that both buyer and seller can do better by trying creative financing than they can by going to a lending institution. In fact these techniques will help you close deals that might otherwise have been impossible.

What happens when you negotiate a second deed of trust with a seller at an interest rate below the prevailing market rate? Lowering your debt service costs makes this a better deal. But how do you calculate the value of the improved cash flow? How do you size up the property's true value under this loan? There are two easy ways, depending on whether or not the loan is fully amortizing (paid off by monthly or otherwise regular payments).

CAPITALIZATION METHOD

For a fully amortizing loan, you simply apply a capitalization rate to the savings in debt servicing — which represents your annual increase in cash flow — and then add the result to the fair market value of the property. That gives you the true value of the property.

As an illustration consider the following loan conditions: (1) a $1 million fully amortizing, low-interest loan that entails $50,000 less in annual debt service than would be dictated by a market-rate loan; (2) a substantial remaining life, say twenty years; and (3) a 10 percent capitalization rate annual yield on the particular property. To discover the true value, simply divide $50,000 by 10 percent. The result — $500,000 — is the added value because as long as the low-interest loan is on the property, you would receive an incremental $50,000 a year in cash flow. Thus the true value of this property under these loan conditions would be $500,000 greater than the property's fair market value.

PRESENT VALUE METHOD

If the loan to be evaluated is not fully amortizing and has to be paid off early with a balloon payment, you cannot use the capitalization rate method. Instead, use the present value method to determine the contribution of the savings in debt service to the property's true value. For example, if a low-interest loan generates an extra flow of income of $50,000 a year for only ten years, at which time a $500,000 balloon payment is due, the present value of the $50,000 a year would be calculated by using a discount rate equal to fair return on money. (Fair return on money is a subjective measure, an informed opinion of market conditions.) The sum total of the present value of the $50,000 in each of the ten years prior to the balloon payment would be the additional value to be added to the property's fair market value.

If the equity build on the low-interest loan is significantly greater than on a market-rate loan, the present
value of the incremental equity build should also be
added to the property's value. Here again, present
value is calculated by using a discount rate equal to
fair return. Thus by adding the present value of both
lower debt service and the equity build to the fair
market value of the property, a seller can determine a
price for the property that reflects the preferential
financing.

The following example illustrates these calculations
for the property described above. For illustrative purposes, assume that fair return on money is 12 percent
and that at the end of ten years, the buyer would have
$100,000 more in equity build than would be avail-
able from market-rate financing:

End of year	Present Value of $50,000 (discount rate 12%)
1	$ 44,643
2	39,859
3	35,589
4	31,776
5	28,371
6	25,332
7	22,617
8	20,194
9	18,031
10	16,099
	$282,511

Discounted value of additional equity build of $100,000 at end of year 10	32,197
Total value of preferential financing	$314,708

A comparison of the two preceding examples shows COMPARISON
that the fully amortizing loan added $500,000 to the
value of the hypothetical property, while the loan with
the ten-year balloon payment added $315,000. Thus
the fully amortizing loan would be preferable for the
seller who is carrying the loan.

One additional point should be considered: If you can assume an existing fully amortizing low-interest loan with a high debt constant (annual payment divided by outstanding debt), the equity build will likely be considerably higher than a market-rate loan, but the cash flow may be even lower. (Here, *high* means 200 basis points or more over the highest conventional first mortgage rate.) When the cash flow is lower, but the equity build higher, you should simply (1) subtract from the property's value the present value of the cash-flow loss, and (2) add to the property's value the present value of incremental equity build. Such loans result from transactions in which the seller is carrying back financing in order to make his or her property more saleable. Obviously, a lending institution would not make a loan at a below-market rate without receiving a substantial equity participation.

VARIABLE-RATE FINANCING, INDEXED TO INFLATION It is impossible to accurately figure the advantages or disadvantages of variable-rate financing without first making assumptions about future rates of inflation. Using your assumptions about interest rates, you can calculate the present value of the future flow of income to the lender over that dictated by the market rate. The sum of all discounted future values of revenues paid to the lender as a result of the assumed increase in payments to the lender should be subtracted from the price of the property.

Assume that the interest rate on a $1 million loan with a ten-year balloon payment will be 14 percent for the first two years, 16 percent for the next two years, 20 percent for the next two, and 22 percent for the last two years. The present value of the loss of revenues above the market rate would be as shown in the table that follows, assuming a fair return of 12 percent and a present lending market rate of 15 percent.

Notice that the variable-rate loan adds value in the initial two years, when it is below the market rate, but thereafter costs money relative to the 15 percent rate. The total to be subtracted from the present value of the

property because of unattractive financing is approximately $119,000.

Year	Present value
1	$ 8,928
2	7,972
3	(7,118)
4	(6,355)
5	(17,023)
6	(15,199)
7	(22,617)
8	(20,194)
9	(25,243)
10	(22,538)
	($119,387)

LONGER-TERM MORTGAGE, INITIAL LOW-INTEREST RATE

If, during negotiations, buyer and seller are unable to agree on the price of the property, but the seller is willing to carry back paper, the buyer can offer a low interest rate (10 percent, for example) for five years, with an optional balloon payment at the end of five years and with the buyer reserving the right to extend the loan for an additional five years (instead of paying the balloon payment) at a substantially higher interest rate (15 percent, for example). The logic here from the seller's standpoint is that the buyer has imposed an onerous penalty on himself if he chooses not to pay off the loan at the end of five years, so the penalty provides an incentive to pay off the loan. In the meantime, the buyer will have the flexibility to either refinance at a lower rate than 15 percent or to extend the loan at the higher rate.

HIGH TAX DEDUCTION FOR INTEREST PAYMENTS

How can a buyer offer a seller a high interest rate and enjoy the consequent high tax deductions without paying a high current debt service? Suppose the buyer wants the seller to carry back $1 million at 10 percent, but the seller wants interest at 16 percent. Both can be accommodated by stipulating that the buyer will pay 10 percent debt service on a current basis and accrue 6 percent to be paid off when the balloon payment comes due. The buyer can take a tax deduction for the full 16 percent if he or she elects to pay taxes on an accrual accounting basis.

If the seller is on a cash basis, he or she does not have to recognize the tax on the accrued interest until the end of the loan. The present-value cost of the accrual liability could be surprisingly low to the buyer. Electing to be taxed on the accrual basis allows the buyer to take current tax deductions for payments to be made sometime in the future; thus, both buyer and seller benefit.

CARRYING BACK
PAPER

How can a buyer convince a seller who wants all cash to carry back paper? One method is for the buyer to give the seller very attractive paper and then find someone who will buy the paper at a discount from the seller. Another way is for the buyer to demonstrate to the seller a method for spreading his or her capital gain over two, three, or four years by carrying back a loan that requires lump-sum payments in each of those years. The seller might benefit from spreading out the capital gain, by remaining in a lower tax bracket and by reducing or avoiding the alternative minimum tax. Spreading out the lump-sum payments allows the buyer additional time to seek financing or to accumulate enough cash to make the lump-sum payments.

BALLOON PAYMENTS

Can a 15 percent loan with a ten-year balloon payment be as advantageous as a 10 percent loan with a five-year balloon payment? I believe that the buyer is almost always better off giving the seller a higher-interest loan with a far-off balloon payment than giving a lower-interest loan with an early balloon payment. There are five reasons for the buyer to do this:

- A far-off balloon payment gives the buyer an opportunity to repay the seller with cheaper dollars from continued inflation.
- The buyer assumes less risk in that he or she is likely to be more easily able to make annual

114   *TACTICAL ECONOMICS*

interest payments than to make the balloon payment when it comes due.

- A high interest rate will cause the building to appear to have low cash flow, or even a negative cash flow, which represents a bargaining point in determining the final price of the property.
- A higher interest rate gives the buyer an opportunity to improve the value of the property if it can be refinanced later at a lower interest rate.
- The after-tax differential cost between 15 percent and 10 percent is only 2.5 percent if the buyer is in the 50 percent tax bracket.

Since having the loan outstanding for five additional years will cost a buyer in the 50 percent tax bracket only 2.5 percent net after-tax per year, he or she can easily justify paying the higher rate. This is particularly true if the buyer is able to negotiate a price reduction as a result of the high interest rate or debt service on the financing, whether from a loan assumption, a seller carry-back, or both.

Chapter Eleven

Determining Return on Real Estate Investments

Comparing apples and oranges is one of the most common pitfalls for investors. Amateurs are easy prey for promoters who conveniently skip over the time value of money. That's because comparisons are meaningless over time unless you factor in the value of the dollar at each stage of the deal. For example, at your investment club someone tells you they bought stock in 1972 worth $200 a share, and now find the issue is worth $400 a share. He concludes that he has a 100 percent capital gain over eight years, or an average of 12.5 percent a year. Furthermore, he explains, his enthusiasm warming, he received dividends of $8 a share for the first four years and $10 a share for the next four years. Thus, the dividends add an average of 4.5 percent per year to the 12.5 percent average capital gain, for a total average (before taxes) of 17 percent a year.

Is he right? Dead wrong. He is comparing apples and oranges. Sure it's all dollars, but the 1972 dollar was worth substantially more than today's dollar. Only when you start looking at the time value of money does it become apparent that the last dollar received in 1980 is a mere shadow of the first dollar received in 1972. With all due respect to your friend's enthusiasm, the apparent rate of return is significantly higher than the true value.

Fortunately there is a technique commonly used by accountants to analyze investments like this one. It's called Internal Rate of Return. Don't let this high sounding phrase intimidate you. It can easily be determined by using any one of a number of programmable financial calculators. It corrects the mistake made by investors who value the last dollar received as highly as the first dollar. In point of fact, the internal rate of return on the stock example cited by your broker is 9.05 percent (excluding dividends) or 12.4 percent (including dividends). The average rate of return calculation of 17 percent is misleading; the internal rate calculation is valid since it considers not only how many dollars are received but also when they are received.[1]

USE INTERNAL RATE OF RETURN—NOT AVERAGE RATE OF RETURN To appreciate the difference between the average rate of return and the internal rate of return, consider the following chart illustrating a $10,000 investment that is worth $40,000 over five, ten, fifteen, or twenty years. The internal rate runs about half the average rate.

	5 Years	10 Years	15 Years	20 Years
Average rate of return	60%	30%	20%	15%
Internal (compounded) rate of return	32%	15%	9.7%	7.2%

Obviously, inadequate or confused methods for determining return on real estate investments can defeat the unthinking investor. Consider a real estate investor who bought a rental house and paid $50,000 for it; he assumed a $40,000 mortgage and put down $10,000. Four years later the property was worth $90,000; by the end of the fifth year, it was worth $100,000. Since he had invested only $10,000, the investor wrongly jumped to the conclusion that he had earned 100 percent during the year when his property increased in value from $90,000 to $100,000. He wasn't thinking clearly. During the fourth year, he had roughly $50,000 in equity in the house ($90,000 − $40,000 mortgage) — not $10,000 in equity. Thus, the return in the fifth year was 20 percent (increase in value ÷ equity, or $10,000 ÷ $50,000) — not 100 percent.

The investor then felt that he should earn more than 20 percent in leveraged real estate, so he decided to sell his property, pay $10,000 in capital gains tax, net $50,000 after tax, and then buy a property worth $250,000. In this way, he would again enjoy 4-to-1 leverage, compared to his current position of $40,000 of debt to $60,000 of equity, or 0.67 to 1. Furthermore, he felt that the $250,000 property had the same chance to appreciate as the $100,000 property. In addition, he calculated that the $100,000 property would have to appreciate 10 percent to give him the same dollar increase in value that the $250,000 property would yield by appreciating only 4 percent. Since both properties could be expected to appreciate at approximately the same rate, there is no question that the investor's decision was a good one. Yields may decline as equity increases — thus the admonition, Beware of diminishing returns.

Suppose you sell a piece of real estate and receive cash and a note receivable in the form of a mortgage. There are two valid ways to calculate the internal rate of return in this case. Let's assume you sell a $100,000 building after having held it for five years. The building has a $60,000 mortgage on it, and you receive a $20,000 cash down payment and a $20,000 second mortgage (second deed of trust) that provides for interest-only payments for six years and a balloon payment in full at the end of the sixth year. Let's further assume that your total investment in the property is $15,000, that the interest rate on the note receivable is 9 percent and that the payments are $1,800 a year (9% × $20,000).

CALCULATING YIELDS WHEN SELLING A PROPERTY FOR CASH PLUS A NOTE

First calculation. One way to calculate the internal rate of return (or compounded rate) is to assume that you can sell the paper to yield, for example, 20 percent, which would require a 41 percent discount. Now your total cash-in-hand is $31,800 (the $20,000 down payment + $11,800 from the discounted paper), which you receive five years after making the initial $15,000 investment. The internal rate of return before taxes is 16.22 percent, exclusive of any tax benefits or cash flow during the holding period and ignoring the tax ramifications of the sale.

Second calculation. Another way to calculate the internal rate of return is to measure the flow of income for the full eleven years, from the time of your purchase through the balloon payment on the six-year note. At the end of the eleven years, your total proceeds would be $50,800 ($20,000 down payment + $10,800 interest on note + $20,000 balloon). The internal rate of return in this case would be 17.69 percent, once again exclusive of cash flow and tax benefits. As you can see, an investor would do better to collect on the note to maturity than to sell the note after discounting it to yield 20 percent.

ALWAYS ATTEMPT TO
FIGURE YOUR
AFTER-TAX RATE OF
RETURN

The investor's most important calculation is the after-tax rate of return, because that represents your net position and properly reflects differences in tax brackets and methods of taxation.

In the earlier example, an after-tax rate of return would be a better guide than the return rate used, which did not consider taxes. For a taxpayer in the 50 percent bracket, the after-tax returns still favor letting the note run to maturity. Consider the sale of the discounted note. Assume the seller pays a tax on 40 percent of the capital gain (after the 60 percent capital gains exclusion). The gain here is $16,800 ($31,800 cash-in-hand − $15,000 original investment), and the taxable gain is $6,720 (40% × $16,800). The total tax is thus $3,360 (50% × $6,720). This tax would have to be paid in April following the fifth year, and the investor's net proceeds, after tax, would be $28,440 ($31,800 − $3,360). The after-tax internal rate of return would be 13.65 percent.

Now consider the case in which the investor holds the note to maturity. Most of the capital gains tax would not have to be paid until the eleventh year, when the balloon payment comes due. The gain on the sale would be $25,000 ($40,000 − $15,000), and after exclusion the investor would have a taxable gain of $10,000 (40% × $25,000). The tax would be $5,000 (50% × $10,000). In this case, the investor's after-tax sales proceeds would be $35,000, and he would have received $5,400 after taxes on the note ($1,800 × 50% = $900 a year for six years). The internal rate of return in this calculation is 14.84 percent.

These after-tax yield calculations also slightly favor the option to let the paper run to maturity. In this example, the after-tax return is a little better than the 1980 inflation rate, 13.2 percent. An investor, however, may feel that he or she should do substantially better to stay ahead of inflation.

Suppose an investor buys a building for $1 million, putting up $300,000 to a $700,000 interest-only first mortgage, and then sells the building for $1.5 million (all cash) five years later. During the holding period, she enjoys 5 percent cash flow, sheltered by depreciation, and she has additional depreciation costs equal to 10 percent of the investment. The investor's basis was reduced during the holding period by 75 percent of the original investment (5 × 15%). She has to pay capital gains on the difference between the $1.5 million sales price and her new basis of $775,000 ($1,000,000 less 75% × $300,000). The internal rate of return, after capital gains tax (assuming her tax bracket is 50 percent) is 19.42 percent.

FRONT-END TAX DEDUCTIONS CAN DRAMATICALLY AFFECT INVESTMENT RETURNS

If, however, our investor had been able to structure her purchase a little differently, she could have substantially improved her return. Suppose she had been able to pay $850,000 for the property ($150,000 to a $700,000 first mortgage) and that she was able to expense out an additional $150,000 paid for repairs and maintenance. Now she sells the building for $1.5 million, and the internal rate of return is 25.78 percent after the capital gains tax (assuming the same amount of depreciation for both examples). The reason for the dramatic difference is that in this case her out-of-pocket expenses are only $225,000, because the tax saving on the $150,000 of repairs is $75,000 (50% × $150,000). A building that requires a lot of repairs and maintenance usually carries a high rate of risk and should yield a higher rate of return upon sale.

In the preceding example, the real estate profit was taxed as a capital gain. Had the benefits been taxed as ordinary income, the net return would have been 13.71 percent instead of 25.78 percent. When an investor takes an ordinary tax deduction and then ultimately pays ordinary income tax on the earnings from the investment, all he or she has accomplished is a deferral of tax, which is not necessarily bad if the deferral is for a substantial period of time. For example, if the deferral were for seven years and the investor earned 10 percent net after taxes on the tax savings, then he would, in fact, ultimately pay his income tax from the net earnings from the tax savings. In other words, he would have had a free ride. Even superior to a deferral of tax is a conversion of an event taxable at ordinary rates into an event taxable at capital gains rates payable in the future. This kind of tax shelter is well worth looking for.

Investors should look for ways to increase their internal rate of return from investments, and they should not give much credence to average rate of return calculations.

Calculations of after-tax internal rate of return are much more informative than before-tax calculations.

A good yield is the result of a good investment, but certain investing techniques also increase yield:

- Shorter holding periods can protect against diminishing returns.
- Front-end tax benefits can increase yield.
- Capital gains treatment enhances investment yield, especially for the higher-bracket taxpayer.

124

¹ The internal rate calculation assumes that all dollars representing the flow of income are reinvested at the same rate as the internal rate. This assumption could be fallacious if you had a high internal rate of return but could not easily reinvest small flows of income into an investment that would provide the same return as the internal rate. The assumption is realistic in the stock example, since the internal rate of return is not very high.

*Chapter
Twelve*

*Reading
Financial
Statements
of Real Estate
Partnerships*

Most real estate investors, and I'm no exception, defer to their accountants when it comes to evaluating the tax consequences of a real estate investment. But even if you've never taken an accounting class, it's important to understand how accountants look at real estate partnerships. You'll do a better job of weighing competing investment opportunities if you apply the same techniques used by the experts.

In my own field of specialization, the limited real estate partnership, obtaining the necessary financial information is simple. That's because government agencies require public program sponsors to spell out whether distributions to investors came from originally contributed capital or money earned through operations. In other words, you can easily find out if a partnership is paying investors out of operating reserves, or from profits earned by the venture.

Before going any further I want to stop for a second **DEPRECIATION** and tell you why public real estate partnerships may be doing better than you think. Even though a public real estate program is profitable, its financial statement may show a loss. That's because of depreciation which shows up on an income statement as an expense and is subtracted from gross earnings. That may seem a little surprising since the sponsor of the program never writes a check for depreciation. It is therefore possible for an investor to have paper losses because of depreciation, while simultaneously earning income. Sound like your kind of deal? Then read on.

Consider a free-and-clear (no debt) building that produces $1 million of gross revenue a year with

$400,000 of cash expenses (not including depreciation) and $700,000 of total expenses (including depreciation). The building would produce an annual operating income of $600,000 but the income statement would show a net income of only $300,000. Investors who do not understand depreciation might wrongly conclude that the investment is earning only $300,000 annually instead of $600,000.

In this case, investors might become more confused if they received cash-flow checks representing dividend income of $600,000 because it would appear that they were getting back their own money. Fortunately, audited financial statements for public real estate programs include a statement of changes in financial position that clarifies what has actually happened to the dollars flowing through the investment. In this simple example, the statement would show $1 million of gross income minus $700,000 of expenses plus $300,000 of depreciation, which would equal $600,000 of net operating income.

Income Statement

Gross revenue	$1,000,000
Operating expenses	400,000
Depreciation	300,000
Net income	$ 300,000

Statement of Changes in Financial Position

Net income	$ 300,000
Add:	
Depreciation	300,000
Funds from operations	$ 600,000
Funds distributed to limited partners	600,000
Funds generated (distributed in excess of funds provided from operations	0

The statement of changes in financial position takes into consideration the fact that depreciation is an intangible expense (one for which no check is written). Thus the program in our example would actually have $600,000 of spendable income to be distributed without depleting the beginning reserves of the program. Investors, therefore, would receive earned dollars rather than originally contributed capital. However, if the program's distributions totaled $700,000, the investor would be getting back $100,000 of originally invested money. This $100,000 would come from reserves and would be reported as "distributions in excess of funds from operations." The future health of a program that made such distributions would be suspect, since the continuation of such a practice would result in the distribution of all the program's reserves. The program would be vulnerable to adverse contingencies that could lead, for instance, to a foreclosure on a leveraged property.

In the example, $300,000 of the distribution would be considered a return of capital and not currently taxable, and $300,000 would be ordinary income. The $300,000 income that was sheltered by depreciation would reduce the investors' cost basis by $300,000.

Assuming that the program uses straight-line depreciation, a capital gains tax results from the difference between the sale price of the property and the cost basis at the time of sale. Cost basis is always reduced by the amount of depreciation taken.

EQUITY BUILD

The concept of equity build (payments of principal on mortgages) also frequently confuses investors reading the financial statements of public real estate limited partnerships. Although equity build appears to be income, the dollars it represents are not tangible and thus not currently accessible. In order to show the real net operational income of a real estate investment program, the statement of changes in financial position specifies the intangible equity build, which has automatically been included as income in the income statement. This statement thus clarifies how much real, tangible operational income was earned; only this tangible income can be distributed to investors as spendable cash flow or used for some other purpose. To illustrate this point, let's return to our earlier example.

The program has $1 million of gross income and $700,000 of expenses (including depreciation). In this instance, let's assume that the mortgage debt on the property requires annual payments of $400,000 interest and $100,000 principal.

Income Statement

Gross revenue	$1,000,000
Operating expenses	400,000
Loan interest	400,000
Depreciation	300,000
Net income (loss)	($ 100,000)

Statement of Changes in Financial Position

Net Income	($ 100,000)
Add:	
Depreciation	300,000
Less:	
Regular principal payments	(100,000)
Funds from operations	$ 100,000
Distributions to limited partners	100,000
Funds generated (distributed in excess of funds provided from operations)	0

The income statement will, of course, show $400,000 of interest expense. But the $100,000 principal payment is not an expense; rather it is a deferred income benefit, assuming the property can be sold for at least the same price originally paid. This $100,000 principal payment — the equity build — has been paid out, but, because it is not subtracted out as an expense, it remains part of net income in the income statement. Consequently, the program's net income is $100,000 larger than its actual cash in the bank. The statement of changes in financial position reflects this difference by subtracting equity build (regular principal payments) from net income. The result of this subtraction is the real spendable and distributable dollars generated by the program. In this illustration, all the distributed income came from operations, and an additional $100,000 net loss was reported.

The income would not be taxable at the time of receipt because it would be considered a return of capital; the investor's cost basis would be reduced by the total amount of depreciation taken. Assuming that straight-line depreciation was used, a capital gains tax would result from the difference between the sale price of the property and the cost basis at the time of sale.

AMORTIZATION OF LOAN DISCOUNT

The income statement includes an item that represents imputed interest on mortgages. This item is often called "amortization of loan discount," which simply means that an expense charge has been made against income when the interest rate on a mortgage is lower than the market rate. An artificial charge (no check is written) is made against income to correct for the possibility that a low interest rate (less than prevailing current rates of between 11.5 and 13 percent) may have been a trade-off for a possible overpayment for the property. Remember, in the statement of changes in financial position, charges or credits to net income would reflect how many real dollars have or have not been spent and how much spendable income is actually available for distribution. The following example illustrates this point.

Gross revenue	$1,000,000
Operating expenses	400,000
Depreciation	300,000
Amortization of loan discount	50,000
Loan interest	400,000
Total expenses	$1,150,000
Net income (loss)	(150,000)

Statement of Changes in Financial Position

Net Income	($ 150,000)
Add (deduct):	
Depreciation	300,000
Amortization of loan discount	50,000
Regular principal payments	(100,000)
Funds from operations	$ 100,000
Distributions to limited partners	100,000
Funds generated (distributed in excess of funds provided from operations)	0

In this example, the program would have a $100,000 cash-flow distribution from operations and a $150,000 tax loss to report.

CONCLUSION The preceding examples have been simplified to illustrate several principles relevant to the understanding of the statement of changes in financial position in public real estate programs. They are intended to help investors determine whether a particular program's operations earned the distributions made or whether the sponsor merely distributed cash from the program's reserves — a distinction that is crucial to understanding the track record and practices of any sponsor of a publicly offered real estate program.

Part
Four

Making
Investment and
Economic
Decisions

Chapter
Thirteen

The
Blumberg
Formula

We've spent considerable time in this book discussing the relative advantages of competing investments such as stocks, bonds, gold, silver and real estate. Obviously there's no such thing as risk free investing. The higher the potential reward, the greater the risk. While that fact of life isn't going to change, it is helpful to know going in what are the comparative risks and rewards. I've devised a comparative reward/risk quotient scoring system, known as "the Blumberg Formula," which can assess this relationship.

The nice thing about the Blumberg Formula is that it quantifies many of the important variables in investment decision making. It also adds a measure of objectivity to your analysis. Although it's hard to predict what will happen to any investment, you can use this formula to help figure out whether an investment is high or low risk.

A key advantage of the Blumberg Formula is that it uses criteria usually not considered by other methods that measure investment opportunities on the basis of risk and reward. Also, it can be applied to any kind of investment opportunity, whereas most methods for measuring risk and reward apply only to stocks and bonds. They also don't attempt to quantify the potential reward in terms of expected after-tax return. Furthermore, most methods used for grading stock and bond opportunities are based on historical information that may be irrelevant to determining real risk/reward ratios. Since the Blumberg Formula measures reward only by potential after-tax return, many high-yielding bonds and stocks held less than a year would get poor reward scores because of taxation at ordinary rates rather than capital gains rates — even if their "beta coefficient" (how they historically perform in good and bad markets) is excellent. Thus, the Blumberg Formula should prove more practical than alternative tools that do not consider taxes and are applicable only to certain investment opportunities. Consider the following examples:

Example 1. Consider an investment in wheat futures with 95 percent of the total purchase price leveraged; in such a case, a movement of only 5 percent would either wipe you out or double your money. By instinct, you would probably assign a risk score of 10 (on a scale of 1 to 10) and a reward score of 10. As we will see later in this chapter, the Blumberg Formula would also assign these scores — for a resulting score of 1.

Example 2. Suppose you have an opportunity to buy government-guaranteed Treasury bills yielding 9.5 percent, and you are in the 50 percent tax bracket. You assume that the risk is minimal, so you give it a risk score of 1. However, the reward, net after taxes, is only 4.75 percent, less than the inflation rate. Thus, the reward would score no greater than a 1. The Blumberg Formula would yield the same scores, for a quotient of 1; so you might as well pass if you are looking for an inflation hedge.

THE "X" FACTOR As the preceding examples suggest, the Blumberg Formula yields trivial results in the absence of information about relevant risk-mitigating factors. To each calculation, therefore, we must add in an "X" factor that represents one or more such risk-mitigating factors. Relevant mitigating measures include: (1) special expertise; (2) special timing; (3) special information; (4) special guarantees; (5) barriers to entry by competition; (6) special management skills; (7) liquidity; (8) nonrecourse financing; and (9) any similar conditions that would tend to protect one's investment capital, including tax benefits.

In the preceding wheat futures example, for instance, suppose that you acquire special information — a close relative in the Department of Agriculture tells you that the Russians have signed a deal to buy 15 percent of the total American harvest in the next few months at a price 16 percent above the current price. This special information from a trusted person might lead you to assign the wheat futures a risk factor of 5. The reward would remain at 10, and the quotient would be 2.

Let us consider a second example of special information. Suppose your oldest and dearest friend tells you that the company he works for has just signed an agreement to recommend to its shareholders a tender offer to purchase the company's stock at $40 a share. Because the stock is now selling at $20, the reward factor might be a 10. The risk factor here depends on the quality of the stock should the merger fall through. If the stock has risen by 50 percent in the last few weeks, the risk might be very large because the stock is likely to drop back once news breaks that the merger negotiations have fallen through. This illustrates the problem with stock market investments in which the motivating force is inside information: if the special information turns out to be less than accurate the individual investor can do little but take the losses.

ADEQUATE CAPITALIZATION

In assessing risk, investors should recall that more investment opportunities fail because of inadequate capitalization than for any other single cause. Unfortunately, adequate capitalization does not guarantee the success of a business venture, as recently demonstrated by a major cigarette company that spent $40 million to advertise a new brand that proved unable to capture even 0.5 percent of the market. However, if adequate capital is an important ingredient to the success of the business and the venture is inadequately capitalized, skip the investment.

NONRECOURSE LOANS

People who own income-producing real estate have learned that during inflationary times properties that represent a break-even investment from a cash-flow standpoint can still bring substantial rewards at the time of sale. If a nonrecourse loan is obtained from a lender or if the seller carries the financing, buyers may have the opportunity to invest one dollar for every three to four dollars at risk by the lender. If the lender has to foreclose, the total remedy is the property and not the personal assets of the buyer-borrower. If a buyer has a purchase money mortgage of three dollars for every one dollar he or she invests, the return on this investment will be four times each percentage point of appreciation; thus, if the property appreciates 5 percent a year, the return would be 20 percent a year when the property is sold. The act of borrowing three dollars for every one dollar invested and not being held personally liable is, in essence, the same as investing four dollars with the possibility of only losing one dollar. This special guarantee or privilege is definitely a risk-mitigating factor.

Many speculators have purchased rental houses with nonrecourse loans even though the houses actually provided a negative cash flow. In the last three years, these speculators have done quite well with this strategy. In the case of the speculator, risk-mitigating factors include (1) full occupancy in the housing stock in the community; (2) tough local controls that are stalling the construction of new housing; and (3) interest rates high enough to inhibit new construction. In such an environment the risk in owning rental housing as an investment is definitely reduced. These mitigating factors can be labeled barriers to entry by competition.

SUBORDINATION AGREEMENTS Another example of a "special guarantee" risk-mitigating factor is illustrated by a case in which one group of investors receives special guarantees from another group of investors in the same enterprise. Perhaps a business needs an infusion of capital and, in order to make the investment more enticing to new investors, the present investors agree to subordinate the return of their own capital on the liquidation of the enterprise to a complete return of capital to the new investors.

This special guarantee would certainly mitigate the risk for new investors because they would be in a position similar to that of bond holders in that their equity would have to be returned before the other equity holders would receive anything. In fact, the new investors' actual exposure cost in the investment is reduced by the amount of value that is being subordinated to their own position.

Clearly, the number of conceivable risk-mitigating factors for various types of investment opportunities is endless. Let us conclude the present discussion of factors by mentioning special forms of insurance that sometimes substantially mitigate risk. For example, Lloyd's of London recently insured computer-leasing companies against default or termination of computer leases, and it now appears that some of the insureds will be paid by Lloyd's for substantial losses. While this is a special case, wise investors will consider these specialized kinds of insurance in assessing risk. Too, certain special issues of municipal bonds and corporate bonds are backed by an insurance company's guarantee that investors will be indemnified in the event of default by the issuer.

Once one has learned to recognize risk-mitigating factors, the next step is to know how to quantify them. The Blumberg Formula for determining the potential success of each investment opportunity can be no more precise than the investor's ability to assign values to the risk and reward factors.

QUANTIFYING REWARDS AND RISKS WITH THE BLUMBERG FORMULA

Reward ratings are assigned on the basis of annual after-tax return:

Reward Rating	Annual After-Tax Return
10	20 percent or better
9	18
8	16
7	14
6	12
5	10
4	8
3	6
2	5
1	4

The reward rating for an investment also serves as the basis from which the risk rating is calculated. (Recall that in the absence of information other than after-tax rate of return, the model assumes risk and reward to be equal.) From this *parity* risk score, then, one wants to subtract the quantified values of any known risk-mitigating factors. Therefore, one first reviews the list of risk-mitigating factors to determine which are applicable: special expertise, special timing, special information, special guarantees, barriers to entry by competition, special management skills, liquidity, nonrecourse financing, tax benefits, and other.

Each applicable risk-mitigating factor is then assigned points based on its importance to the success of the enterprise:

- Factor is of *minor* importance   0.5 points
- Factor is of *major* importance   1–2 points
- Factor is of *crucial* importance   3 points

These points are then subtracted from the parity risk score to yield the risk rating. Only assets guaranteed by the federal government or a federal agency ever receive an unqualified risk score of 1.

Take the following example: An investment opportunity arises that has the potential to yield 20 percent a year after taxes. Its reward score, then, is 10. Your assessment of the risk-mitigating factors enables you to reduce the parity risk score from 10 down to 3. The investment's Blumberg Formula quotient would be 3.3 — reward appears to be 3.3 times the risk — which suggests a worthwhile opportunity:

After-tax rate of return	20 percent
Reward rating	10 points
Parity risk score	10 points
Risk-mitigating factors	
Special timing	3
Special expertise	2
Special management skills	2

| Risk rating | 3 points |
| Quotient (Reward ÷ Risk) | 3.33 |

Additional risk-mitigating factors pertain to investments that provide tax-shelter benefits. The most important rule here, however, is that the quality of the investment itself is always paramount; tax-shelter benefits, while certainly relevant to the attractiveness of an investment, are secondary advantages.

TAX-SHELTER BENEFITS

Tax-shelter benefits can mitigate risk — but the greater the shelter, the higher the risk. Usually, the more leverage involved in a tax shelter, the higher the potential write-off and also the higher the risk. Since the revenue acts of 1976 and 1978, the IRS has been restricting the ability of the investor who is seeking a tax shelter to benefit from leverage without having personal recourse on the debt. Leveraged real estate remains the only investment still available to the investor on nonrecourse financing.

Another factor that must be considered is how long a tax-sheltered investment can be extended before a taxable event is realized. The longer an investment can be stretched out (if it is failing), the better for the tax-sheltered investor because he or she retains the use of the potential tax money while waiting for the taxable event to occur.

A third relevant factor is whether the taxable event occurs as ordinary income or as capital gain. Under the Economic Recovery Tax Act of 1981, a capital gain is far preferable to ordinary income, since ordinary income from an investment can be taxed at a rate as high as 50 percent whereas the maximum capital gains tax is 20 percent. In other words, for a taxpayer in the 50 percent bracket $100 of ordinary income is worth only $50 after taxes, while $100 of capital gains is worth $80.

Consideration of the above three factors yields the following quantification rule. If the investment could be stretched out at least seven years should it go bad, a risk-mitigating factor worth between 1 and 2 points should be assigned. The reason I use seven years as a holding period is that I assume I can invest the tax-saved dollars at 10 percent after tax, in which case they will double in approximately seven years. Therefore, my use of the government's money will allow me to pay taxes from earnings I would not have had if I did not use the tax shelter. The exact point value of this consideration varies with higher write-off and shorter holding periods, or lower write-off and longer holding periods; the investor will have to decide if the benefit of the write-off is worth 1 or 2 points according to his or her own tax situation. There is one exception to this rule: if there is an extraordinarily high write-off (in excess of 200 percent) and no recourse on the debt, 3 risk points should be subtracted if capital gains tax treatment will be applied when the taxable event occurs.

Some deep tax shelters (over 300 percent) may yield a high internal rate of return even if the investor receives only half his original capital investment. This will usually occur if the investor's taxable event happens when he is in a very low tax bracket and he takes the deductions in a very high tax bracket. It will always occur if the taxable event is realized as a capital gain. If the write-off is to be recaptured as ordinary income after seven years and the write-off is over 300 percent, 3 risk points should be subtracted.

INTERPRETING BLUMBERG FORMULA QUOTIENTS A quotient between 3.0 and 5.0 constitutes an excellent inflation-hedge opportunity. As Figure 9 illustrates, few investments fall in this range. If an investor applies the Blumberg Formula to evaluate many investment opportunities and discovers that a majority of these opportunities fall between 3.0 and 5.0, it is likely that he or she is assigning scores either too high on the reward scale, or too low on the risk scale, or both. For in the final analysis, the scores are a function of how liberal or conservative the investor's own investment beliefs and attitudes are.

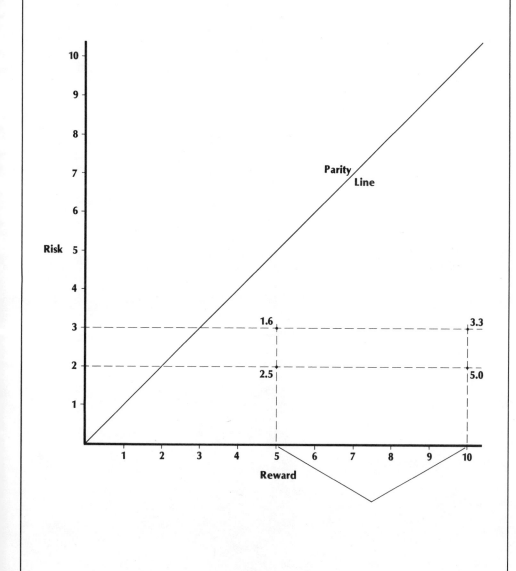

Figure 9.

Evaluation Grid for the Blumberg Formula

Chapter Fourteen

The Investment Lull Before The Investment Explosion

Throughout this book we've emphasized the pivotal role that inflation plays in tactical investing. There's no question that real estate outperforms stocks in periods of high inflation. Likewise, stocks outperform real estate during periods of relative price stability. The big question now is how will stocks and real estate perform over the next couple of years?

Obviously anyone who has the answer to this question will have an advantage when it comes to making investment decisions. Let's take a moment to examine recent financial history in the United States. Over the past five decades both stock and real estate values have exploded in stairstep fashion. In the case of stocks, the first explosion following the recession of the thirties took place during World War II. Because houses, automobiles and luxury items were simply not available, people had no place to put their money. That's why they chose to invest in stocks. But in September of 1946 the market crashed, remaining rather lackluster until the early fifties, then exploding in the mid-sixties, crashing again in the late '69-'70 recession, and then literally exploding again in the period August '82 to the present. In the case of real estate, values exploded right after World War II, then again in the late 60's and 70's. A generalization one can make regarding stocks and real estate is that they both moved in stairstep fashion to higher price values.

Since August 1982 we've witnessed the American Exchange Index, the NASDAQ Index and the Wilshire Composite Index of 5,000 stocks increase close to 100 percent. On the other hand, we've seen real estate prices present a very mixed picture.

The price of apartment houses has increased dramatically while the prices of office buildings and shopping centers have lagged. Interestingly, the price of resale homes has also just barely stayed ahead of inflation. Could this mean we are at the flat part of the stair for real estate and the top of the vertical part of the stair for stocks? I think not, and the reader will notice a definite bias for buying both stocks and real estate at this particular time.

In 1972, when the Dow Jones Average was trading in the 800 range, we all thought that we would be looking at a 1600 Dow Jones Average by the year 1982, because all that would be required would be an 8 percent compounded growth rate. As it turned out, in the decade of the 70s we had inflation growing at a compounded rate of 8 percent, while the Dow Jones Average was growing at a compounded rate of roughly 2 percent.

If one looks at the real value of the Dow Jones Average after inflation, from 1973 through the beginning of 1983, one would have to assume that the Dow Jones should be at 1600 in order to equal the buying power of an 800 1973 Dow Jones Average. Since the Dow is trading today at about 1250, it should be apparent that the Dow has to increase approximately 30 percent just to *equal* the buying power of 1973. This argument lends credence to the proposition that we are on the horizontal part of the stair rather than on the vertical part. The time to have purchased 3M Co., Polaroid Corp., Fairchild Camera, Texas Instruments, Inc., and a host of other great market performers was not in 1969 when they hit their highs, but rather in the 1950s when they were growth stocks with a great future.

Stocks of this nature typically go through three stages. In the first stage, they may command multiples of 30 to 100 times their earnings just based on the sheer rush of optimism about what could be if their special products turn out to be winners. During stage two, the multiples still will remain high if you are fortunate enough to run into a bull market and the potential of the company is actualized in earnings and revenues. During stage three, which is when the company runs into a bear market and reality sets in, you're lucky if you can give the stock away at 15 times earnings. The old adages about the stock market, "Even a turkey can fly in a strong wind", and "When they raid the cathouse they take the madam, too" are valid. In other words, even poor stocks do well in an up market, and even good stocks suffer in a down market.

It seems to me that right now we are completing the first year of a bull market. Statistics show that in every economic recovery accompanied by a stock market recovery, the bull market has averaged two and a half years. If this holds true, we are still on the flat part of the stair, and there are probably opportunities galore in stage one still to be picked up. Because of the plethora of research and development partnerships which were formed over the last three or four years and which are now bringing their companies public and the innumerable privately owned companies that now wish to go public, I don't think the big question will be, "Are there any opportunities left?" but instead, "Which ones to choose?" There's no question there will be some long-term winners in the group, but there will be many short-term winners.

For those investors who are not reluctant to take short-term gains because they have a way to shelter the ordinary income, this is probably a fine time to invest. Since we now have an alternative minimum tax, taking short-term gains doesn't seem quite as onerous because one can shelter them with tax-advantaged investments and thereby avoid the tax. Unfortunately, the same is not true with long-term capital gains because the nonexcluded portion of the capital gain is taxed at up to 50 percent and cannot be sheltered, except with long-term capital losses.

Just as there are many companies in stage one which can be bought either as new or recent issues, there are many stage two companies that have not yet enjoyed their full potential in this most recent market surge. What must be apparent for the companies to be selected is 1) a comparative product advantage, and more importantly, 2) there should be something unique about the company or the product or both. In the case of 3M Co., they were the first ones with cellophane tape. In the case of Polaroid Corp., they were the first with instant pictures, and in the cases of Fairchild Camera and Texas Instruments, they were among the first with semi-conductor technology. These are the kinds of companies where the big rewards justify the risk. If we are in stage three, we can all wait to buy the growth companies of tomorrow because they'll be a lot cheaper in a few months. Since I don't believe stocks in stage two are going to have to face stage three (a bear market) for at least another 18 months, I think the reward/risk ratio is excellent for buying growth stocks at this time. Investors who do not have the time or inclination to pick individual stocks should be buying growth mutual funds in a family of funds, so they can easily switch into cash when stage three hits.

WHERE ARE WE IN THIS CYCLE FOR REAL ESTATE INVESTMENT? Investors interested in taking advantage of the current phase of the market in real estate should ask themselves: 1) What kind of real estate? and 2) How much longer is this phase likely to last? My opinion is that this is an excellent time to be buying housing, and particularly multifamily dwellings, even though the price will be dear. I firmly believe that smart money is buying existing multifamily dwellings right now and not building new ones. While I believe we're on the lower part of the vertical portion of the stair, I also believe there's plenty of room left in the apartment house appreciation cycle, at least 36 months. Consider the following evidence for my enthusiasm: In '72, apartment house occupancies were at approximately 90 percent, and we built 1.2 million apartment units and 1 million new homes that year; in 1983 we are building only 600 thousand multifamily units and the demand for new housing, including single family dwellings, is estimated to be between 1.5 million and 1.7 million new units, which just equals the current annualized rate of new construction. In 1972, a nice family home could still be purchased for under $35,000; today, in most parts of the country, the same home would probably cost more than $80,000. In 1972, approximately 75 percent of the people in the family formation age group could afford a home; today it is estimated that less than 25 percent of the family formation age group can afford a home. Since the population in America has grown by better than 20 percent since 1972 to 233 million, and since the national occupancy rate for apartments is better than 95 percent in most parts of the country and the ease of exit from apartments is substantially diminished because of the unaffordability of a single-family dwelling, it seems to me that apartments represent an excellent reward/risk ratio purchase today. When you consider the Accelerated Cost Recovery accounting rules as they affect apartments, the argument is substantially enhanced. This is true because apartments currently represent the only form of real estate in which 15-year, 175 percent declining balance depreciation can be taken with only the accelerated portion to be recaptured as ordinary income. All other forms of real estate require that 100 percent of the depreciation taken be recaptured as ordinary income when accelerated depreciation is used.

I am also very bullish on the purchase of office buildings and shopping centers at this time, because they can be bought substantially below replacement costs and at capitalization rates close to historical highs for this kind of investment. For example, it is not unusual to buy a shopping center today at cap rates ranging from 10 to 12 percent. The reason these prices appear to be bargains today is that shopping centers and office buildings were the hardest hit by the recent recession. In addition, in many parts of the country such properties were overbuilt and occupancy rates are less than 85 percent. For many of the new complexes, the break-even point is 90 percent occupancy, so these complexes are losing money. Office buildings and shopping centers realize their highest value at the high point of an economic recovery. Since it's hard to say how strong the economic recovery will be, buyers of shopping centers and office buildings may have to wait longer for their profits than buyers of apartment complexes. (As a point of interest, the economic recovery from 1975 to the end of 1979 lasted 59 months.)

There are many other forms of real estate one could consider, such as mobile home parks, industrial property, combination industrial and office building property, land leaseback purchase, and purchase leaseback of business properties. The business type of property responds more to the state of the economy than anything else, whereas, housing investments respond to factors such as family formation numbers, new construction numbers, the affordability of single-family dwellings and, of course, interest rates, that do not necessarily have anything to do with the economy. One of the reasons I'm most bullish on apartments today is that I believe the chance for rapid rent increases is the greatest for that type of real estate. All other forms of real estate are more dependent upon the state of the economy and the length of term of leases that are currently associated with the property.

CONCLUSION I think by now the reader must suspect that I am quite optimistic about the prospects for the future of the economy; I believe the next 24 months will be an outstanding growth period for the United States. I believe that in 1984 we will see a relaxing of interest rates and an increasing amount of new tax legislation to help reduce the deficit. The Federal Reserve will be encouraged to take its foot off the monetary brakes as Congress shows increasing willingness to increase taxes and reduce expenditures. Today, there are numerous investment opportunities that are on the horizontal part of the stair, and the reward/risk ratio for many of them favors the potential for reward. There are many companies in the fields of biomedicine, energy, and technology, in areas such as defense, robotics, biotechnology, information storage, space technology, ocean technology and food technology, all of which are in the early one and two stages. Those companies that will be the super successes of the late '80s and '90s will get clobbered during stage three, and some people will hang on and be vindicated. Some will sell and be sorry, and some will sell and buy them back later. Since timing has as much to do with overall return as picking the right stock, I hope we will all be smart enough to sell early in stage three and buy back the next time the stock is in stage two, when the stock looks cheap.

Where real estate is concerned, there are considerations other than perfect timing, since real estate is not as liquid as stocks and since there are tax and refinancing considerations which are pertinent to real estate and not to stocks. For example, it might be better to refinance a property than to sell it, thereby avoiding a taxable event. If you refinance the property, you may find that you will realize almost as much cash as if you sold it, and you can still enjoy the appreciation. You might even decide to trade up the property in order to get a new depreciation base while postponing a large tax bite that would occur if you sold the property. While I believe real estate should be looked at as a longer term investment than stocks, I also believe that when circumstances beyond your control are endangering the value of your property you should sell it or trade it quickly, regardless of tax ramifications. To sell, refinance or trade up a piece of real estate every two or three years is probably one of the best ways to build the real estate side of your portfolio quickly. To sit with one piece of real estate until the mortgage is paid off and hold it free and clear might be okay if your objective is to maximize income, but it is very poor strategy if your objective is maximize net worth.

The one admonition I would make regarding both stocks and real estate is that you not invest because somebody else tells you it's a hot item; you should, instead, do a very thorough examination yourself before making the purchase so that you will have the conviction to hang on when you should be hanging on and to sell when you should be selling. In the final analysis, nobody has more interest than you in doing the right thing, since it is your gain or loss that will go to the bottom line.

Chapter
Fifteen

Formula
for
Economic
Turnaround

In our democratic nation most people are put off by the notion of a double standard. What's true for one should be true for all. Ironically, if we are to make a real economic turnaround, slash unemployment and fund necessary public services, we may need to go to a two-tier interest rate system. This novel concept could lead to affordable credit for targeted markets, while maintaining a damper on inflation. My suggestion will not please those who fear government intervention. Yet, this could be a creative government approach leading to prosperity throughout the 1980s.

Why is the two-tier interest rate system so important? To understand this, it's necessary to see what it will take to turn the economy around. Specifically we need to have

- short-term rates drop to a level that causes consumers to buy on credit;
- the allotted $200 billion defense budget substantially spent;
- an increasing percentage of the work force open individual retirement accounts;
- the tax cuts mandated by the Economic Recovery Tax Act of 1981 remain in effect without substantial Congressional modification; and
- the Federal Reserve loosen the reins on the money supply.

Of course, all these conditions, except the third (IRA investments), are demand oriented and therefore inflationary. But one hopes that when they have all come to pass, the inflation rate will be low. For example, if inflation were to increase from 4 percent to 6 percent, it would be relatively tolerable, considering the inflation level we have experienced over the last five years.

Arguments about whether demand-side or supply-side economic theories are most appropriate at this time miss the point — they resemble debates about which of the scissor blades cuts the paper. Clearly, elements in both supply-side and demand-side formulas are right. Supply-siders hold that lower taxes and incentives will stimulate the economy. Demand-siders believe that cutting taxes at the expense of an unbalanced budget will push up interest rates and slow recovery. But when consumers, business owners, lenders, and borrowers all expect continued high rates of inflation, interest rates never get a chance to come down, regardless of whether demand-side or supply-side economic policies are in effect.

Interest rates will drop significantly only when people believe that the economy is stable, which means when they perceive that there is little or no federal deficit. Deficit spending either compels the Fed to print more money, which is inflationary, or forces the Treasury to borrow, which pushes up interest rates. If the budget is balanced, neither of the distasteful alternatives — printing money or borrowing to fund deficits — is necessary.

In this chapter, I propose a series of recommendations to enhance the economic recovery now underway. My analysis of how interest rates affect the economy is followed by specific proposals concerning the federal budget, the monetization of the debt, the Federal Reserve's method of reporting the money supply, and federal subsidies for housing and automobile loans.

INTEREST RATES AND ECONOMIC HEALTH

Supply-side theory holds that if people increase savings there will be money available to fund the federal deficit, consumer borrowing, and business needs — all while interest rates drift to a more reasonable level.

162

The theory may be proved correct someday, if savings ever increase to the desired level. But we cannot wait to find out, nor can the economy remain healthy while we sit hoping that savings increase.

John Rutledge, economist with Claremont Economic Associates, points out that a dollar's worth of taxes is a more efficient way to fund the budget than a dollar's worth of deficit funding, because a dollar's worth of deficit funding in effect imposes a "tax" on all the securities "that came before." In other words, excess printing of money is inflationary, which in turn reduces the value of all fixed debt instruments. In addition, since private-sector borrowing competes with government securities, one can assume that the additional "tax" is paid in higher interest costs to both the producer and the consumer.

Since 1976, the average cost of borrowing money has doubled for most companies. Higher interest rates have significantly affected both the prices of merchandise produced and the earnings of the producers. To see how interest rates affect earnings, consider this example: Assume a corporation has (1) a capitalization of $100 of debt and $100 of equity; (2) pretax earnings of 10 percent on its capitalization (or $20); and (3) a historic average of $10 in interest costs. If the cost of interest doubles, the corporation's pretax earnings are halved.

	Historic Interest Rate	Historic Rated Doubled
Capitalization	$100 debt at 10%	$100 at 20%
	100 equity	100 equity
	$200	$200
Pretax Earnings	$200	$200
	10%	10%
	$ 20	$ 20
		(10) additional
		interest
		$ 10

One way for this company to maintain profits is to raise prices, but in a recessionary economy that is very difficult. Consequently, even a strong corporation is forced to reduce earnings, while a weak, undercapitalized corporation goes into the red or files for bankruptcy. Obviously, highly leveraged corporations are those most likely to be forced out of business. Unfortunately, these are the young corporations that may have the greatest future in the areas of innovation and technology. Their failure would be seriously detrimental to the economic future of this country.

Now consider an example that shows how interest rates affect pricing. If historically the average cost of borrowing money was 7 percent but the cost suddenly jumped to 14 percent, just to maintain its past earnings a company would have to raise its prices 1.75 percent, assuming it turned inventory over four times a year ($4 \times 1.75\% = 7\%$ additional interest cost). While this 1.75 percent may not seem dramatic, such an increase can drastically affect competitiveness in international trade.

When the price of credit doubled in the United States, compared to an average increase of less than 50 percent for other developed nations, the U.S. was put at a serious competitive disadvantage in the pricing of goods and services. In addition, high interest rates in the U.S. tend to strengthen the dollar. In real (i.e., inflation-adjusted) terms, between June 1980 and June 1983 the dollar increased 75 percent against a composite index of the ten leading Western industrialized nations' currencies (see Chapter 3). High interest rates thus create a double disadvantage for the U.S. in its trade with other nations. Finally, it is very difficult for producers to sell durable goods to credit buyers when the cost of credit is prohibitive.

Clearly, then, the net result of high interest rates can be recessionary. Business failures are increasingly frequent. The Department of Commerce predicts that 80 of every 10,000 businesses will go out of business in

1983. This rate is the highest since the 1930s, when 100 of every 10,000 businesses failed. The high cost of money has significantly contributed to this economic duress.

The real question now is: How can we possibly drop interest rates without producing excessive rates of inflation? The answer is that inflation will remain under control only if the public believes that the growth of the money supply is being properly restricted and the federal government seems likely to balance its budget.

Our economy works best when the following economic conditions exist: consumers have buying power; there is full employment; and business is operating near full capacity. Unfortunately, even if these three conditions hold, the federal government still can foul up the system by spending far more than the tax revenues collected, as it did in the 1960s and 1970s to finance the Vietnam War.

THE $1 TRILLION FEDERAL DEBT

In 1960 the national debt was $26 billion; it has now surpassed $1 trillion. (If the federal debt were a stock, this compounded rate of growth of 20 percent would have been a great investment.) The ratio between the gross national product (GNP) and total federal debt has remained fairly constant, but the cost of maintaining the debt has risen rapidly as compared to the total federal budget — debt maintenance accounted for approximately 16 percent of the 1982 budget, compared to 13 percent in 1979. This cost not only crowds private industry out of the debt market but also exacerbates the problem of balancing the budget. Furthermore, the average duration of the Treasury obligations has been roughly halved (to approximately 2.75 years) in the last five years. At the same time, the average interest rate on the debt has almost doubled — to more than 10 percent.

BALANCING THE BUDGET

Fiscal policy leads monetary policy as the most important factor determining interest rates — an unsurprising conclusion reached in a recent study by the Minneapolis Federal Reserve. There is no way that the Federal Reserve can provide lower interest rates over the long term, because in a free marketplace inflation expectations ultimately determine interest rates, and these expectations will not come down until the deficit is greatly reduced. Thus despite Congress's resolution in 1975 that mandated the Fed to stipulate its targets and make every effort to maintain them, the real responsibility for interest rates finally lies with Congress and whether it controls government spending. But Congress has been unwilling to authorize fiscal restraint in two of the largest budget items: Social Security and defense.

Congress has instead discussed special excise taxes on luxuries, such as alcohol and cigarettes, a tax surcharge on incomes of over $35,000, and the exclusion of interest deductions for all consumer loans except home and auto financing. Although such measures could raise new tax revenues, they cannot compensate for the deficits generated by bloated defense budgets and a ballooning Social Security liability. Furthermore, the "inflation tax" can be far more deleterious to the economy than a real tax because of how it influences people's thinking about money and because of the effect it has on our ability to compete in world markets. Clearly, if long-term economic stability is desired, Congress must play a role in cutting spending.

Assuming a strong recovery, three measures should suffice to cut the projected deficit in half for fiscal 1984 and probably balance the budget in 1985:

- Index future changes in Social Security payments to equal 50 percent of the annual percentage change in the consumer price index (CPI).
- Impose a special value-added tax of 2 percent at retail level only.
- Reduce budgeted spending for defense by 10 percent.

Sometimes monetizing the debt is an appropriate economic remedy. When the Fed finances debt by buying Treasury investments directly, it is in effect simply printing money. This process adds to the money supply and can be inflationary. High inflation, for example, resulted from monetizing the debt incurred during the Vietnam War. Monetizing the debt during that period, however, was not part of a coordinated and controlled program of economic growth — it was merely a way of paying for the war that seemed less painful than asking the American people to accept higher taxes.

In contrast, a controlled monetizing of the debt can provide a stimulus to economic growth by making credit more readily available for expanding plants and equipment, for construction of new housing, and for financing purchases of consumer durables such as automobiles. These effects, in turn, cause more people to be employed and fewer people to be receiving transfer or entitlement payments, and more money is available to consumers for purchases. The danger of monetizing the debt is that if the increasing money supply is not matched by increased productivity, inflation will ensue.

Alternatively, when the Treasury sells its instruments directly to the public, instead of selling them to the Fed, a depressing influence on the economy can result, because interest rates stay high and the amount of funds available to consumers and industry is reduced. In effect, the U.S. government "crowds out" other borrowers. Data from the Federal Reserve illustrate how borrowers have been increasingly "crowded out" by the Fed's failure or refusal to monetize a larger portion of the debt:

	Federal Deficit (in $ billions)	Purchases of Debt by Fed (in $ billions)	Percentage of Deficit Monetized
1973	7.9	9.2	116%
1974	10.9	6.1	56
1975	75.1	8.5	11

Formula for Economic Turnaround

	Federal Deficit (in $ billions)	Purchases of Debt by Fed (in $ billions)	Percentage of Deficit Monetized
1976	56.6	9.8	17
1977	50.9	7.1	14
1978	43.8	6.9	16
1979	28.1	7.7	27
1980	67.8	4.5	7
1981 (nine months)	24.3	1.6	6

If debt is monetized during the heart of a recession, the action is relatively palatable to those monetarists who fear high inflation. If debt is monetized in the heart of a growth year, inflation expectations are much greater. As in every economic decision, timing is of the essence. When the nation is coming out of a recession, it is the right time to monetize a larger portion of the debt. Done in the correct proportion, the effect on the economy will be salutary.

REPORTING THE MONEY SUPPLY Every week the Federal Reserve reports on the money supply. Often the figures represent aberrations beyond the Fed's control. Indeed, the Fed cannot control the money supply from week to week because the variables that affect the money supply are unpredictable. So, one week M-1B (demand accounts, currency, and NOW accounts) may be up 10 percent on an annualized basis; the next week, down 10 percent on an annualized basis. Tremendous uncertainty colors the relationship between the M-1B measure and the real conditions of money supply. Furthermore, M-1B does not reflect the current situation because there is a two-week delay in reporting.

Nonetheless, for a week in which the money supply is reported to have grown at an annualized 10 percent, the Fed comes under great pressure from the Administration to tighten credit. The Fed often overreacts by pulling "excess reserves" out of the system — thereby raising the federal funds rate (the rate banks charge each other for overnight loans). The Fed may also raise the discount rate (the rate the Fed charges member banks), add a surcharge to the discount rate, as it did in 1981, or modify reserve requirements of the entire banking system — each of which has the same effect as pulling excess reserves out of the system.

To avoid overreactions, the Fed should report the M-1B monthly, instead of weekly and provide the annualized rate for both that month and the preceding twelve months as well. Such reports would give a far more realistic picture of money supply than the weekly peaks and valleys that are, by and large, uncontrollable by the Fed.

For example, current weekly reports are distorted for the first week of each month, when Social Security recipients receive their checks and the monetary aggregates, in turn, tend to grow more rapidly than normal. Monetary aggregates also tend to grow beyond the Fed's control when major mergers take place, because the cash involved in these transactions is borrowed. Similarly, when large sums of Euro-dollars enter this country the monetary aggregates grow inordinately in the week the cash transfers take place.

By instituting a more logical and less disruptive method for watching the monetary aggregates, the Fed could prevent knee-jerk reactions. Ultimately, interest rates might come down faster simply because the reports would be more meaningful, and money dealers would not be sitting on the edges of their seats every Friday wondering which way to jump. I believe that a more reasonable method of reporting the money supply could knock 200 basis points off both the federal funds rate and the prime rate.

There will be enormous pressure on the Reagan administration to raise taxes to reduce the deficit. Unfortunately, increased taxes would nullify much of the incentive to produce or invest. It would be far healthier for the government to subsidize cheaper credit for automobiles and housing. Increased production in all businesses affected by the construction and auto industries would increase federal and state tax revenues and make a balanced budget realizable. Consider the following analysis.

COMPETITIVE MARKET THEORY OF INTEREST RATES As we observed in Chapter 1, the traditional relationship between inflation rates and interest rates is no longer valid. Up through the 1970s long-term lenders followed a rule of thumb that set long-term interest rates 3 percentage points above their expectations for inflation. Institutional short-term lenders were guided by a lower prime rate, usually reserved for their best customers, which they set arbitrarily, based on supply and demand. When the annual inflation rate dropped to as low as 3.5 percent early in 1983, many expected that the old rule of thumb would be applied and that long-term rates would fall substantially.

In the latter half of the 1970s, however, a new trend developed: the normal "yield curve" became inverted; that is, short-term rates actually surpassed long-term rates. In 1979, we watched the prime rate hover around 20 percent while long-term rates were in the mid teens. A new "competitive market" theory emerged, according to which supply and demand — and not yield curves — determined the relationship between inflation and interest rates. In December 1981, the St. Louis Federal Reserve published an extensive study indicating that competitive market theory had become the dominant model in the determination of interest rates.

Why such a change in the nature of the money markets? As one might suspect, there is no single cause, but a combination of factors.

- During the 1970s the U.S. Federal Reserve greatly accelerated the pace at which it printed money. The costs of higher oil prices and of financing the war in Southeast Asia were both paid for by inflating the dollar, thus raising both the actual rate of inflation and inflation expectations.

170

- In October 1979, the Fed embarked on a policy of letting interest rates float as they would and concentrated its efforts instead on controlling the money supply.
- Because it was easier for corporations to float debt than equity, businesses borrowed heavily through bond issues and corporate commercial paper, causing disintermediation (the removal of capital) from banks and thrifts.
- Borrowers' demand pushed rates to new highs almost every other month. It became obvious to Americans that borrowers were being rewarded and savers penalized by the combination of the tax system and high inflation.
- The Monetary Controls Act, enacted by Congress in March 1980, deregulated Regulation Q (to be phased out by 1986), which had set limits on what bank and thrift institutions could pay on savings and certificates of deposit. The act further allowed thrift institutions, previously restricted to real estate loans, to diversify by placing up to 20 percent of their assets into other investments, such as commercial paper and consumer and commercial loans.
- Further deregulation since 1980 now permits thrift institutions to make consumer loans with almost the same latitude as banks.

As we have seen, current high interest rates are helping to hold down inflation and are contributing to a strong and stable dollar. At the same time, considerably lower interest rates are needed if we are to have a healthy housing industry and revived durable-goods industries. As long as we choose not to monetize debt (i.e., print money) for fear of more inflation, we must continue to finance current federal debt by issuing Treasury bills and certificates.

CAN WE EASE THE ECONOMIC HARDSHIP CAUSED BY HIGH INTEREST RATES?

Significant reductions in interest rates in the near future are highly unlikely, given the current demand for money. Yet high borrowing costs dampen eco-

PROPOSAL FOR A TWO-TIER INTEREST-RATE SYSTEM

nomic development, which in turn keeps unemployment high and hinders real economic growth. One solution would be a two-tier interest rate system subsidized by the federal government. Local and state governments and some federal agencies already, in effect, subsidize a two-tier system by considering revenue from certain bond issues to be tax-free.

Recall, too, that for many years the federal government has been in the subsidy business. It has at times subsidized (1) farmers for what they produced and what they did not produce; (2) airlines by protecting certain routes; (3) dairy producers by guaranteeing a fixed price for their goods; (4) oil and gas producers by guaranteeing a fixed rate for their production; and (5) housing for the poor and the aged by guaranteeing loans and below-market interest rates. All these programs were designed to serve a worthwhile purpose, although each eventually came to be viewed by many as stifling competition and being counterproductive to economic growth.

But government subsidy is not an unmitigated evil; it has often proven of value in our economy. The extraordinary success of the U.S. farming industry, for example, is attributable to government protection of farm prices in tough times. Similarly, the housing and construction industries thrived on the indirect subsidies they received in the forms of government loan guarantees for mortgages and the tax-deductible status of interest. Moreover, the reason U.S. self-sufficiency in meeting our energy needs has risen to 50 percent is our subsidy of the oil industry by allowing price fixing, depletion allowances, and tax deductions for intangible drilling costs.

Thus federal subsidies have long been an effective economic strategy. The key questions are *when* to subsidize, *what* to subsidize, and *how* to subsidize. The current high levels of real interest rates suggest that the time has come for a two-tier interest rate system, one tier of which would be partially subsidized.

If federal subsidies enabled home buyers to obtain mortgages at lower interest rates, the economic benefits of new home construction and purchase would more than exceed the costs the government would incur in making the subsidies. Economists tell us that a drop of a percentage point in the unemployment rate will yield approximately $20 billion in federal net revenues. Their estimate is based on the taxes that will be paid by the reemployed, the decrease in entitlement payments, and the taxes generated by the buying power of new workers.

The arithmetic of such an interest subsidy program is simple. Using housing as an example: the government could borrow $20 billion at 10 percent and lend it at 8 percent; the subsidy would in effect cost $400 million (2% × $20 billion). The $20 billion would finance the construction of 85,000 housing units at a cost of $100,000 each if 70 percent financing were provided. Assume that 30 percent of the cost of each unit represents the cost of labor. Then $6 billion would be paid to newly employed construction workers. These wages would be subject to federal income tax at an average rate of 20 percent, yielding new income taxes of $1.7 billion. Bottom line — the government would have invested $400 million in interest subsidies, and it would see a return of $1.7 billion in increased taxes. From anyone's perspective, a 400 percent return on invested capital isn't shabby.

INTEREST RATES AND OUR STANDARD OF LIVING

The future prosperity of American industry and the economy depends on how we adapt to absorb all the dollars printed since 1969, when we last had a balanced budget. Since the dollar is the medium of exchange in Western international trade, the stability of the dollar is a matter of international concern. Yet, our domestic interest is to stimulate the housing industry and other durable goods, such as automobiles, to assure real economic growth for our economy. Furthermore, housing and transportation are critical elements of our standard of living, which according to the Organization for Economic Cooperation and

Development (OECD), far exceeds that of other developed nations, including Japan. (Recent OECD statistics show that Japan's per capita standard of living is only two-thirds of the U.S. standard. Figures for other Western nations are even more startling.)

Thus it makes sense for our federal government to create policies to stimulate two industries — housing and automobiles — with enormous impact on our standard of living. Some, however, say that since the U.S. has lost its competitive advantage in building cars, we should let the automotive industry wither. Others say that young people should no longer hope to own their own homes. But the auto and housing industries have done very well in the last thirty years, and even after the roughest of times in the last two years they are still the cornerstone of the American economy. In the future, cars and homes may well be smaller, but they will be financed, built, and sold until other industries grow large enough to absorb their shrinkage; otherwise, we will only watch our economy regress.

I'm convinced the United States can experience real economic growth at an annual rate of 4 to 5 percent for the rest of the decade, even in the face of high interest rates. However, this will happen only if the government nurtures key industries during times of high real interest rates.

ECONOMIC GROWTH MAY REQUIRE A TWO-TIER SYSTEM

If we want both real economic growth and a stable dollar, then we are asking for growth in an environment of relatively high interest rates. To make this happen, the government may have no choice but to create conditions that enable more people to buy cars and homes — that is, to make lower-interest consumer credit available through federal subsidies or state revenue bonds.

The construction industry, with its relatively high percentage of unskilled and semiskilled laborers, can

174

employ the unemployed faster than any other industry. What better way to stimulate consumer spending than to put hundreds of thousands, perhaps millions of people back to work? But the housing and construction industries can expand only if less-expensive credit is available for home buyers.

As we have seen, a balanced federal budget and a controlled, predictable money supply are necessary to lead the economy out of a recession into steady growth. In turn, these achievements would favorably influence public perception, which itself can substantially affect interest rates, consumer buying, investment, and capital expenditures. If the government firmly demonstrates an intention to balance the budget and control the money supply, an economic turnaround can begin even before these primary goals are achieved. The budget does not have to be balanced all at once. Public belief that a balanced budget is possible can in itself stimulate capital formation.

There is a delicate balance between the amount of money in the economy and the resulting economic growth and inflation (see Figure 10, pg. 176). When a nation is unable to employ its people, and its productive capacity is operating at 70 percent — as is now the case in the U.S. — pragmatic prescriptions are needed to put people back to work and exploit full industrial capacity.

The tax cut and all the economic incentives in the Economic Recovery Tax Act of 1981 will not save the auto and housing industries as we know them unless there is affordable credit. In order to have economic growth, we must have productive housing and auto industries, at least until we have developed other basic industries that can employ similar numbers of Americans.

Real economic growth will materialize only when there is the proper incentive to produce, and that will

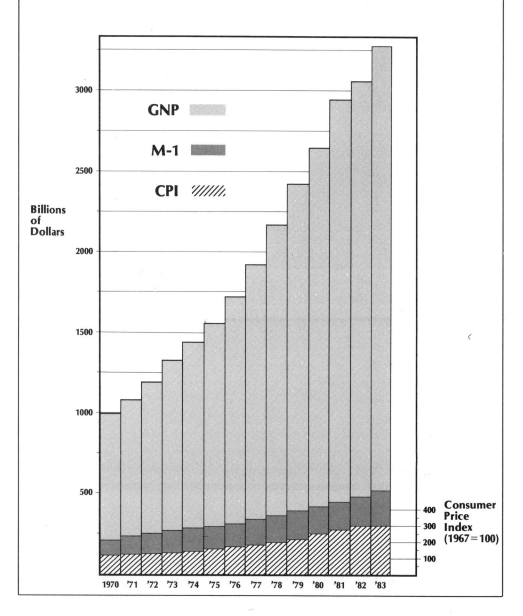

Figure 10.

Money Supply (M-1), Consumer Price Index (CPI) & Gross National Product (GNP),
1970-1983

*Sources: U. S. Department of Commerce
Economic Report of the President*

GNP

M-1

CPI

Billions
of
Dollars

3000

2500

2000

1500

1000

500

Consumer
Price
Index
(1967=100)

400
300
200
100

1970 '71 '72 '73 '74 '75 '76 '77 '78 '79 '80 '81 '82 '83

176

happen only if there is enough consumer demand. For this reason I propose that we need to keep asking the following three questions: How is the government going to finance the deficit — monetize or sell Treasury instruments directly to the public? How much do we really want to spend on defense? How can we resurrect two of our largest industries — auto and housing? Only by wisely answering these questions can we hope to achieve the delicate balance between economic growth, price level, and money supply.

Glossary

Accelerated cost recovery.
A method for determining annual deductions on real estate and other capital assets that allows for larger deductions in the early years and for straight-line depreciation. (See *Depreciation*).

Accelerated cost recovery system (ACRS).
A system provided under the Economic Recovery Tax Act of 1981 (ERTA) to determine deductions available on capital assets such as real estate; includes straight-line depreciation as well as accelerated cost recovery.

Accelerated depreciation.
Methods of depreciation that recognize amounts in excess of straight-line depreciation during the initial years of the asset's useful life. Various methods of accelerated depreciation are allowable for federal tax purposes, but upon the sale or other disposition of the asset they result in the recapture of ordinary taxable income equal to amounts depreciated in excess of that allowable for straight-line depreciation. The excess of accelerated depreciation over straight-line depreciation is considered an item of *tax preference* with respect to real property. If the taxpayer is not a corporation, such excess depreciation claimed with respect to leased personal property is also an item of tax preference. (See *Depreciation, Accumulated depreciation,* and *Straight-line depreciation.*)

Accumulated depreciation.
Sum of depreciation taken using either straight-line or accelerated depreciation methods. (See *Depreciation, Accelerated depreciation,* and *Straight-line depreciation.*)

Alternative minimum tax.
Created under the Revenue Act of 1978, this federal income tax is calculated on the total of taxable in-

come plus the excluded portion of capital gains and excess itemized deductions. The alternative minimum tax, which does not apply to corporations, is applicable only to taxable years ending after 31 December 1978. The tax rate is graduated (after an exclusion of $20,000), from 10 percent to a maximum of 25 percent. Not an add-on tax, it is paid only in the amount that exceeds the sum of the regular federal income tax and the add-on minimum tax. Certain investment tax credits may not be used to reduce the alternative minimum tax.

Amortization.
The gradual reduction of a debt by means of equal periodic payments sufficient to meet current interest and liquidate the debt at maturity. When the debt involves real property, often the payments include tax impounds and hazard insurance on the property.

Appreciate.
To grow or increase in value.

Appreciation participation mortgage (APM).
A mortgage through which the lender participates in the appreciation of the property by exchanging a reduction in the mortgage interest rate for a percentage of equity in the property. The mortgagee shares in the appreciation at the time of loan payoff or sale.

Assumption of mortgage.
The taking of title to property by a grantee, wherein he assumes liability for payment of an existing note secured by a mortgage or deed of trust against the property; becoming a co-guarantor for the payment of a mortgage or deed of trust note.

At-risk provisions.
Provisions in the Tax Reform Act of 1976 that severely limit deductions from tax shelters by restricting deductions to amounts "at risk," which is defined to exclude borrowed amounts (1) with respect to which an investor has no personal liability; (2) from related persons or those with an interest in the activity; and (3) protected against loss by guarantees, stop-loss agreements, and similar arrangements. Real estate, how-

ever, is exempt from the at-risk provisions, and real estate investors can continue to realize tax and economic advantages of nonrecourse financing.

Balloon payment.
A final, large installment payment whose sum exceeds that of the preceding installment payments and repays in full a note.

Basis.
An asset's original cost, in most cases, which may later be adjusted; a capital gain results when selling price exceeds basis.

Blind pool program.
A tax-sheltered program that at the time of its inception has not yet allocated the proceeds of the offering to specific purposes, projects, or properties.

Bond.
A promissory note issued by a corporation, government agency, or the like whose terms include a fixed rate of interest to be paid to the bondholder for a fixed period of time, when the face value of the bond will be repaid.

Capital gain.
Income that results from the sale of a capital asset (e.g., stocks, bonds, collectibles, real property held by someone other than a "dealer") at a price above tax basis. Usually refers to long-term gains (from sale of asset previously held by seller for more than one year). For federal tax purposes, short-term capital gains are treated as ordinary income; long-term capital gains are subject to a lower effective tax rate in that the Revenue Act of 1978 permits the exclusion of 60 percent of the net long-term capital gains received after 31 October 1978; the remaining 40 percent is taxed as ordinary income.

Capital contributions.
The sum of all investors' contributed capital in a real estate investment program without the deduction of selling expenses or outlay for the operation or organization of the program.

Capital improvement.
Improvement or replacement of a capital asset that is expected to produce benefits beyond one year.

Cash flow.
The reported net income of a corporation plus the sum of indirect expenses (costs not paid in actual dollars) such as *depreciation* and *depletion*.

Charitable remainder annuity trust.
A trust with a charity as ultimate beneficiary, where annual sums are paid to an individual during his or her lifetime in fixed dollar amounts or amounts that are a percentage of the initial value of the trust.

Charitable remainder unitrust.
Similar to a *charitable remainder annuity trust,* except that the annual sums may be a fixed percentage of the trust's value as that value is redetermined every year.

Clifford trust.
A trust lasting more than ten years, after which the property reverts to the original creator.

Collateral.
The specific property that a borrower pledges as security for repayment of a loan.

Consumer price index (CPI).
An index, compiled by the U.S. Department of Labor, that measures the cost of a typical wageearner's purchases of good and services.

Convertible security.
A security that may be exchanged by the owner for another security in accordance with the terms of the issue.

Creative financing.
Innovative techniques for financing a major investment purchase by reducing cash outlay and increasing leverage.

Crummey trust.
An irrevocable life insurance trust designed to permit premiums to be paid with dollars that are given to the trust free of gift taxes.

Debt service.
The regular payments of principle or interest required by terms of a note or contract.

Deduction.
An item that may be subtracted from taxable income, the taxable estate, or taxable gifts, thereby lowering the amount subject to taxes.

Deferral.
A form of tax shelter that results from an investment that offers deductions during the investor's high-income years, and postpones capital gains or other income until after retirement or during another period of lower income.

Demand/supply ratio.
A measure of the net market demand for a product, commodity, or the like; calculated by dividing market supply by market demand.

Depletion.
A tax deduction granted developers of oil, gas, and other natural resources to encourage exploration for new deposits and development of new supplies by permitting partially tax-free recovery of the costs of exploration and development activities.

Depreciation.
The allowable tax and accounting deduction for the amortization of the actual cost of improved property over its useful life. An indirect expense, in that no cash outlay occurs. Depreciation is assumed, for tax and accounting purposes, to represent the utilization of assets expected to exist beyond one year, even though the assets may be appreciating in value. Land is considered to have a perpetual life and, therefore, only the improvements are considered depreciable.

Development loan.
A mortgage loan to finance all or part of the cost of the acquisition of land (including leaseholds) and the development of the land into finished sites, including the installation of utilities, road, drainage, and sewage systems, and other improvements prior to construction.

Direct reduction mortgage (DRM).
A direct reduction mortgage is liquidated over the life of the mortgage in equal monthly payments. Each monthly payment consists of an amount to cover interest, reduction in principal, and, in some cases, taxes and insurance. The interest is computed on the monthly outstanding principal balance: as the principal balance is reduced, the amount of interest decreases, thereby providing a larger portion of the monthly payment to be applied to the reduction of principal.

Discretionary trust.
A trust in which an individual gives a broker or someone else discretion (either complete or within specific limits) as to the purchase and sales of securities.

Diversification.
(1) The spreading of investments among different companies in different fields. (2) The participation of an individual company in a wide range of business activities.

Double taxation.
Refers to the treatment of corporate profits, which are first taxed as corporate income, and then the part distributed as dividends to stockholders may be taxed again as income to the recipient stockholder.

Dow-Jones averages.
Widely quoted and regularly computed averages of closing stock prices. They include an industrial stock average, a rail average, a utility average, and a combination of the three.

Economic Recovery Tax Act of 1981 (ERTA).
Among its provisions, ERTA raised transfer tax exemptions and tax-free gift amounts, lowered tax rates, and introduced the unlimited marital deduction.

Elasticity.
The ability of a bank to meet credit and currency demands during times of expansion and to reduce the availability of credit and currency during periods of overexpansion.

Employee Retirement Income Security Act (ERISA).
The pension reform act, passed in 1974, that established federal standards for private pension plans concerning levels of coverage.

Employee stock ownership plan (ESOP).
A plan by which a percentage of the ownership of a private corporation is held by the corporation's employees; also known as a *Kelso plan*.

Equity (property).
The difference between a property's current market value and the owner's current debt.

Equity build.
An increase in the equity of a real estate investment due to reduction (amortization) of existing loans by payments of principal. The cash value of equity build is not realized until the sale and collection of sales proceeds of a property for a price at least equal to its original cost or until the refinancing of a property for an amount at least equal to the original mortgage.

Equity dollars.
The actual cash outlay to the seller at the time of purchase, including cash deposits paid to the seller prior to the close of escrow that are attributable to the purchase price of the property.

Equity kicker.
Provision for a lender's equity participation in a real property as an inducement to lend funds.

Equity trust.
A real estate investment trust (REIT) that acquires income-producing properties, as contrasted with a mortgage REIT, which makes or purchases loans on real estate.

Escalation clause.
A provision in a lease that allows increases in rent when the landlord's actual costs rise or with the occurrence of other economic events agreed to in the lease, such as changes in the consumer price index (CPI).

Estate.

All assets owned by an individual at the time of death. The estate includes all funds, personal effects, interests in business enterprises, titles to property — real estate and chattels, and evidences of ownership, such as stocks, bonds, and mortgages owned, notes receivable.

Estate tax.

Tax imposed by the federal government and some states on the estate of a decedent, taxing the decedent's privilege of leaving his or her property to others.

Estate trust.

A trust that is formed as a holding place for a decedent's possessions; usually used to facilitate the passage of funds from one generation to the next.

Fair market value.

The price a willing buyer would pay a willing seller if neither was under any compulsion to buy or sell. The standard at which property is valued for estate tax.

Federal Deposit Insurance Corporation (FDIC).

A corporation established by federal authority to provide insurance on demand and time deposits in participating banks up to a maximum of $100,000 for each depositor.

Fannie Mae.

Familiar form for Federal National Mortgage Association certificate. A real estate oriented security, whose holders are guaranteed payment of interest and principal by a United States government agency, the Federal National Mortgage Association.

Federal Housing Administration (FHA).

An agency of the federal government that insures loans on residential property.

Federal Savings and Loan Insurance Corporation (FSLIC).

A corporation established by federal authority to provide insurance for savings and loan deposits.

First mortgage.

A mortgage that usually takes priority over other liens upon the same real property and that must be satisfied before any other claims on the proceeds of a property sale.

First mortgage loan.
A loan for which a first mortgage is used as security or collateral.

Fiscal year.
A twelve-month period used for accounting and tax purposes; need not coincide with the calendar year.

Fixed interest.
An interest rate that does not vary and is guaranteed for the duration of the investment term.

Fixed liability.
Any *liability* that will not mature within the ensuing fiscal period; for example, long-term mortgages or outstanding bonds.

Foreclosure.
A legal process whereby a mortgagor of a property is deprived of his interest therein, usually by means of a court-administered sale of the property.

Foreign exchange.
Usually refers to the trading in or exchange of foreign currencies in relation to United States funds. Rates of exchange are established and quoted for various foreign currencies based on the demand, supply, and stability of the currency.

Freddie Mac.
Familiar form for Federal Home Loan Mortgage Association certificate. A real estate oriented security, whose holders are guaranteed payment of interest and principal by a United States government agency, the Federal Home Loan Mortgage Association.

General partner.
The individual (or individuals) having unlimited liability in a partnership. Usually distinguished from a limited partner in tax-shelter investments, the general partner secures the proper income-producing properties and has the responsibility of managing them on a profitable basis.

General partnership.
An entity whose partners are jointly and severally liable for partnership obligations.

Gifts to Minors Act. (See *Uniform Gifts to Minors Act*.)

Ginnie Mae.
Familiar form for Government National Mortgage Association — GNMA — certificates. A real estate–oriented security, whose holders are guaranteed payment of interest and principal by the United States government, representing portions of a pool of government-guaranteed Federal Housing Administration (FHA) and Veterans Administration (VA) mortgages. Unlike bonds, Ginnie Maes do not pay back the principal at maturity; instead, principal is repaid each month with the interest. (*Freddie Mac*, like Ginnie Mae, sells its own government-insured bonds and uses the proceeds to buy either insured or conventional mortgages from federally insured savings and loan associations.)

Gold bullion.
Bars of gold that can be purchased on world markets with little markup. Their utility as an investment vehicle is limited by minimum purchase requirements, delivery and storage costs, and lack of liquidity.

Government bond.
An indebtedness of the U.S. Treasury. Considered the safest type of security available.

Graduated-payment mortgage.
A creative financing technique in which the payments gradually increase at a predetermined rate, as the borrower's earning power increases or is anticipated to increase. The earlier payments are lower than those that would be required by fixed-rate or variable-rate mortgage financing.

Gross multiplier.
A method of evaluating property that analyzes a property's income compared to that of similar properties in the same or comparable market area. The gross rent

multiplier (GRM) is a property's price divided by its rent.

Growth investment.
The center portion of the *investment pyramid,* between the foundation and speculative investments; usually includes mutual funds, managed equities, and stocks, among others.

Hard asset.
An investment that is tangible, as opposed to paper or intangibles; for example, metals, gems, art, stamps, and collectibles.

Hedging.
A purchasing strategy used by dealers in commodities and securities, manufacturers, and other producers to prevent loss due to price fluctuations. A present sale or purchase is counterbalanced by a purchase or sale of a similar commodity, or a different commodity, usually for delivery at some future date. The desired result is that the profit (or loss) on a current sale or purchase will be offset by the loss (or profit) on the future purchase or sale.

Hypothecated account.
An account that is pledged or assigned as collateral for a loan; for example, savings accounts, trust accounts, and the like.

Hypothecation.
An agreement that permits a creditor to foreclose on the collateral pledged to secure a loan in the event that the loan is unpaid at maturity. When a borrower arranges for a second loan and pledges collateral as the security for the loan, he or she must sign a hypothecation agreement, usually included in the note, that empowers the bank to take possession of the securities to realize payment of the loan in case of default.

Hypothecation loan.
A loan secured or collateralized by an existing mortgage loan, but without the retirement, reconveyance, or sale of the existing loan.

Individual Retirement Account (IRA).

A tax-deferred retirement account that may be established by any individual under the age of 70½ who has earned income (wages or salary). Annual contributions are limited to $2,000 ($2,250 if a second account is established for a nonworking spouse). Contributions are deducted from taxable income, and contributions and their earnings are not taxed until the funds are withdrawn. Various stipulations govern the types of investments that may be made, penalties for withdrawals before age 59½, and the like.

Inflation.

A condition of increasing prices, usually caused by an undue expansion in paper money and credit.

Installment sale.

A sale complying with special rules that allow the capital gain resulting from the sale to be realized (and therefore taxed) over the period during which the payments are actually received.

Interest.

Payments made by a borrower to a lender for the use of the lender's money, or by a depository institution to a depositor, or by a corporation to its bondholders.

Interim loan.

Any loan for the purpose of funding the development or construction of real estate.

Inter vivos.

(Latin, "between living persons.") Describes a trust, transfer, gift, or the like made during a person's lifetime.

Investment pyramid.

A formula devised by James Barry for identifying the mix of investments in an individual portfolio. The average mix includes 10 to 20 percent each in low-risk (foundation) investments and high-risk (speculative) investments. The remaining 60 to 80 percent should be in moderate-risk (growth) investments.

Joint tenancy.
Co-ownership between two or more people with right of survivorship. Because a survivor automatically becomes the owner of a decedent's interest, this arrangement avoids probate.

Joint venture.
A form of business organization in which the participants share jointly in the ownership, management authority, and liability. (In contrast, see *limited partnership.*)

Kelso plan.
(See *Employee stock ownership plan.*)

Keogh plan.
Tax-deferred retirement plan for self-employed persons and partners, named after Congressman Eugene J. Keogh, who introduced them in a 1962 bill. Annual contributions are limited to the lesser of 15 percent of self-employment income or $15,000. Various rules govern withdrawals, penalties for early withdrawals (before age 59½), and the like.

Lease.
A contract between owner and tenant, setting forth conditions upon which tenant may occupy and use the property, and the term of the occupancy.

Lease option.
A creative real estate financing technique in which the buyer, for a consideration, leases a home with the option to buy later. In most cases, a portion of the monthly payments and the consideration are applied to the purchase price.

Leaseback.
Upon purchase of a real property, the practice of leasing the property back to the seller for a definite time period, requiring the payment of cash-on-cash returns. (The *cash-on-cash return* is the amount paid the lessor on the leaseback.) When extended over long periods of time, a leaseback is similar to providing a

loan to the seller, with the property as collateral. When utilized over short periods of time, a leaseback is an often-used method of obtaining a seller's guarantee of cash flow during the start-up operations of a newly developed property.

Lessee.
A person or entity who enters into a contractual relationship to use property owned by another. (In real estate, commonly referred to as a *tenant*.)

Lessor.
An owner of a property who allows another person or entity to make use of that property under a contractual relationship. (In real estate, commonly referred to as a *landlord*.)

Leverage.
The use of borrowed money (debt) in relation to equity; a highly leveraged real estate transaction carries a large percentage of financing.

Liability.
Any claim against a corporation; for example, accounts and wages and salaries payable, dividends declared payable, accrued taxes payable, and fixed or long-term liabilities, such as mortgage bonds, debentures, and bank loans.

Lien.
A claim against property that has been pledged or mortgaged to secure the performance of an obligation. A bond may be secured by a lien against specified property of a company.

Limited partner.
Passive investor who has limited personal liability in a partnership. (See *Limited partnership*.)

Limited partnership.
An entity whose partners include one or more general partners and one or more limited partners; records a certificate of limited partnership with the proper authorities.

Liquidation.
(1) The process of converting securities or other property into cash. (2) The dissolution of a company, with the cash remaining after sale of its assets and payment of all indebtedness distributed to the shareholders.

Liquidity.
The ability of the market in a particular security to absorb a reasonable amount of buying or selling at reasonable price changes. Liquidity is one of the most important characteristics of a good market.

Living trust.
A trust established by an individual during his or her lifetime; same as *inter vivos trust*.

Loan constant.
A rate that refers to the annual periodic payments on an amortizing loan (i.e., principal and interest). For a given sum, the loan constant will be lower with a lower interest rate or a longer loan term. Conversely, the loan constant increases with a higher interest rate or a shorter term.

Lock-in clause.
A provision in a note prohibiting prepayment.

Locked-in.
Description of an investor who is unable or unwilling to realize a profit by selling a security because the profit would immediately become subject to the capital gains tax.

M.A.I. appraisal.
An appraisal by a member of the American Institute of Appraisers.

Mortgage.
An instrument by which the borrower (mortgagor) gives the lender (mortgagee) a lien on real estate as security for a loan. The borrower continues to use the property, and the lien is removed when the loan is repaid.

Mortgage bond.
A bond secured by a mortgage on a property. The

value of the property need not necessarily equal the value of the bonds issued against it.

Mortgage REIT.

A real estate investment trust (REIT) that specializes in either making or buying permanent mortgage loans or providing short-term (interim) financing or long-term financing for construction and development projects. (See *Real estate investment trust.*)

Municipal bond.

A bond issued by a state or a political subdivision, such as a county, city, town, or village. The term also applies to bonds issued by state agencies and authorities. In general, interest paid on municipal bonds is exempt from federal income taxes and from state and local income taxes within the state of issue.

Mutual fund.

An open-end investment company that continuously offers new shares to the public in addition to redeeming shares on demand as required by law.

Net lease.

A lease in which the tenant (lessee) pays the real property taxes and operating expenses, and the landlord pays for major improvements and debt service.

Net, net lease.

A lease in which the tenant (lessee) pays the real property taxes, operating expenses, and insurance, and the landlord pays for major improvements and for debt service.

Net, net, net lease (triple net lease).

A lease in which the tenant (lessee) pays all costs of ownership, including debt service, and the landlord's responsibilities are limited to major improvements to the property.

Nonrecourse debt.

A loan that, in the event of default, limits the remedies of the creditor to recovery of stated collateral (i.e., land and improvements) and prohibits a personal judgment or other recourse against the owner for any deficiency caused when the property is liquidated to satisfy the loan balance. The repayment of a non-recourse debt is secured only by the real property involved.

Occupancy rate.
The percentage of occupancy of an income property. Calculated for multifamily housing as the number of rent-paying units divided by the number of rentable units on a given date. Calculated for commercial or industrial properties as the number of square feet leased divided by the number of leasable square feet on a given date.

Open-end investment company.
An investment company that has outstanding redeemable shares. Also generally applied to those investment companies that continuously offer new shares to the public and stand ready at any time to redeem their outstanding shares.

Open-end mortgage.
A mortgage that secures additional advances which a lender may advance to the mortgagor.

Option.
A right to buy or sell specific securities or properties at a specified price within a specified time.

Partnership.
A contract between two or more persons to unite their property, labor or skill, or some part thereof, in pursuit of some joint or lawful business, and to share the profits in certain proportions.

Percentage lease.
A lease in which the rental includes a percentage of the volume of sales, receipts, or income, usually in addition to a guaranteed minimum.

Points.
Amounts paid to a lender as a loan fee. For federal income tax purposes, points must be amortized over the term of the loan — except in the purchase of homes, in which case points are deducted when actu-

ally paid, so long as such payment of points is an established business practice in the area in which the indebtedness is incurred and the amount of the payment does not exceed the amount generally charged in that area.

Prepaid interest.
The payment of advance interest on a loan. Such prepayments are deductible for federal income tax purposes only on an accrual basis, that is, in the taxable years for which the interest expense accrues.

Prepayment privilege.
A provision in a note, resulting from the use of the words "or more," or other similar language, giving to the mortgagor the privilege of paying all or part of the unpaid balance of the note at any time without penalty.

Present value.
The discounted value of a certain sum due and payable on a specified future date.

Prime rate.
The lowest interest rate on business loans, available only to a bank's largest customers.

Principal.
(1) The person for whom a broker executes an order, or a dealer buying or selling for his or her own account. (2) An individual's capital. (3) The face amount of a bond. (4) The property comprising a trust; synonymous with *corpus and res*.

Principal and Income Act.
A uniform act in force in most states, determining what items of receipt or payment are either principal or income.

Pro forma.
(Latin, "according to form.") In financial planning, usually used to refer to an analysis done by a professional regarding the prediction of tax or other financial obligations.

Pro forma projection.
Statement of the anticipated operating income and

expense of property based on assumptions about various financial factors.

Pro forma rent.
Estimated rental income for an income property; based on an "as if" basis; for instance, estimated gross income at an apartment complex is estimated as if rental prices were increased to uniform, projected market levels and actually collected as of a given date on a given type of unit.

Promissory note.
A negotiable instrument that is evidence of a debt contracted by a borrower from a creditor. If the instrument does not have all the qualities of a negotiable instrument, it cannot legally be transferred from one person to another.

Property and casualty insurance.
Insurance coverage to provide for the replacement of or compensation for property lost, stolen, damaged, or destroyed.

Prospectus.
The document by which a corporation or other legal entity offers a new issue of securities to the public.

Proxy.
A shareholder's written authorization that nominates someone else to represent his or her interests and assume voting rights at a shareholder's meeting.

Prudent man rule.
An investment standard. In some states, the law requires that a fiduciary, such as a trustee, may invest the fund's money only in a list of securities designated by the state — the so-called legal list. In other states, the trustee may invest in a security if it is one that a prudent man of discretion and intelligence, who is seeking a reasonable income and preservation of capital, would buy.

Public program.
A tax-sheltered program that is registered with the Securities and Exchange Commission and distributed in

a public offering by broker or dealers, or by employees of the sponsor. Public programs are commonly, but not always, organized as limited partnerships.

Purchase money loan.

A loan used for the purchase of real property. The lender can be either the seller or a third party. Because the real property acts as the sole collateral for the loan, in the event of a default there usually is no personal liability to the purchaser-borrower.

Real estate.

Raw land, residential and low-income housing, and other income-producing properties, such as office buildings, shopping centers, and industrial and commercial properties. Real estate is the most widely used form of tax shelter; benefits are derived principally from: deductions for depreciation and interest, leverage, and capital gains. Real estate investments are available through both public programs and private programs.

Real estate investment trust (REIT).

An equity trust that can hold income properties of all types and offers shares that are publicly traded. A REIT is a modification of a limited partnership that does not require net worth or income minimums for the investor.

Recapture of depreciation.

The inclusion as ordinary income of the excess of accelerated depreciation over straight-line depreciation, with respect to real property, and of all depreciation taken with respect to personal property. Recapture of depreciation occurs upon the sale or certain other disposition of property.

Recourse.

The rights of a "holder in due course" of a negotiable instrument to force endorsers on the instrument to meet their legal obligations. The holder in due course must have met the legal requirements of presentation and delivery of the instrument to the maker of a note, and must have found that this legal entity has refused to pay for, or defaulted in payment of, the instrument.

Regulation Q.
The regulation extended by the Federal Reserve Board that places a limit on the rates of interest that can be paid by banks to their depositors.

Regulation T.
The federal regulation governing the amount of credit that may be advanced by brokers and dealers to customers for the purchase of securities.

Regulation U.
The federal regulation governing the amount of credit that may be advanced by a bank to its customers for the purchase of listed stocks.

Replacement cost.
The estimated cost of replacing the capital improvements on an operating real property, together with estimates of depreciation based on such cost. It is based on the lowest amount that would have to be paid in the normal course of business to construct a new asset of equivalent operating or productive capability. Such estimates generally do not reflect a property's current market value and are sometimes figured on a square-footage basis in regard to constructing a comparable new building in the same geographical area, with reference to published indices.

Repurchase agreement.
An agreement between seller and buyer that the seller will buy back the note, security, or other property at the expiration of a period of time or upon the completion of certain conditions, or both.

Reserves.
The portion of the original *capital contributions* of investors to a real estate investment program that is not invested in property but is set aside to provide for contigencies, deferred maintenance, and expenses for major repairs and replacements.

Return of capital.
A distribution to an investor from a source other than net income as determined for tax or accounting pur-

poses. For tax purposes, a return of capital is not taxable.

Return on investment.
Rate of pretax profit earned in relation to the value of a shareholder's original invested capital; stated as a percentage of the original purchase price and referred to as *yield* when a shareholder owns a small portion of the equity of a particular, usually large, investment.

Revenue Act of 1978.
Provisions of this federal income tax act include: (1) reduction from 50 percent to 40 percent the amount of an individual's net capital gains that are subject to ordinary income tax rates; and (2) elimination of the excluded portion of net capital gains as an item subject to the minimum tax on tax preference items, which reduces the amount of personal service income eligible for the 50 percent maximum tax. Capital gains received after 31 October 1978 are subject to an *alternative minimum tax*.

Revenue bond.
A municipal bond backed by revenues produced from a particular project, such as a turnpike.

Revocable trust.
A trust that may at any time be revoked or amended by its creator.

Risk factors.
In real estate investment programs, unpredictable factors that could affect real estate values; for example, changes in, or rulings on, federal or state tax laws; government regulations affecting rents, fuel, energy, or environmental factors; changes in interest rates and in the availability of long-term mortgage funds; changes in the neighborhood of the properties acquired or in the area's competition; and possible default by lessees in purchase or leaseback transactions. The program's sponsor should warn all prospective investors about relevant risk factors.

Rule of 72.
A simple financial formula for calculating the amount

of time it will take an investment to double at a given rate of return: divide the rate of return into 72.

Second mortgage.
A creative real estate financing technique in which the buyer maintains the original mortgage and "takes back" a second mortgage on the difference between the down payment and the existing first mortgage. Thus, a form of seller financing.

Secondary mortgage market.
The activities of lenders selling their mortgages in bulk, with continually fluctuating interest rates.

Secured loan.
A loan that is secured by marketable securities or other marketable valuables. Secured loans may be either time (of specified duration) or demand loans (may be called at any time). (See also *Hypothecation*.)

Securities.
Any stock, shares, voting trust certificates, bonds, debentures, notes, or other evidences of indebtedness, secured or unsecured, convertible, subordinated, or otherwise; or any warrants, options, or rights to subscribe to, purchase, or acquire any of the above.

Securities Act of 1933.
A federal act regulated and enforced by the Securities and Exchange Commission (SEC) whose provisions require the registration and use of a prospectus whenever a security is sold publicly (unless the security or the manner of the offering is expressly exempt from such registration process).

Securities Exchange Act of 1934.
A federal act regulated and enforced by the Securities and Exchange Commission (SEC) that supplements the Securities Act of 1933. Contains requirements designed to protect investors and to regulate the trading of securities in open-market trading (secondary market). Such regulations require, among other items, the use of prescribed proxy statements when investors' votes are solicited; the disclosure of management's and large shareholders' holdings of securities; con-

trols on the resale of such securities; and periodic (monthly, quarterly, annual) filing with the SEC of financial and disclosure reports of the issuer.

Securities and Exchange Commission (SEC).
An independent federal government regulatory and enforcement agency that supervises investment trading activities and registers companies and those securities which fall under its jurisdiction. The SEC also administers statutes to enforce disclosure requirements designed to protect investors in securities offerings.

Self-liquidating loan.
A short-term commercial loan, usually supported by a lien on a given product or commodities, that is liquidated from the proceeds of the sale of the product; for example, a loan granted for the growing of crops.

Sponsor.
An entity that acts as a general partner, manager-operator, or management company of a tax-sheltered program.

Soft real estate (or rental) market.
A condition under which there is a substantial vacancy rate in the market area.

Sprinkling trust.
Synonymous with *discretionary trust*; so called because the trustee can "sprinkle" the income among various beneficiaries.

Step-up interest payments (variable interest rates).
Variations in interest rates prescribed to occur at specified times, as opposed to fixed-term interest rates or those that vary with independent economic indicators.

Stock.
Ownership shares of a corporation.

Stock certificate.
A certificate that provides physical evidence of stock ownership.

Stock dividend.
A dividend paid in securities rather than cash. The dividend may be additional shares of the issuing company or shares of another company (usually a subsidiary) held by the issuing company.

Straight-line depreciation.
The recognition of depreciation in equal annual amounts over the estimated useful life of an asset. (See *Depreciation, Accelerated depreciation,* and *Accumulated depreciation.*)

Straight loan.
A loan granted an individual, or other legal entity, in which the basis for granting the credit is the borrower's general ability to pay; a loan unsupported by any form of collateral security.

Subchapter S corporation ("S" corporation).
A corporation electing to be taxed as a partnership, which allows the flow-through of tax consequences to the owners as partners.

Subordination agreement.
An agreement by which a third party grants a bank a priority claim or preference to the assets of the borrower ahead of any claim that he or she may have. When more than one legal entity has an interest or claim upon the assets of a prospective borrower, a bank may require that the other interested parties sign subordination agreements before a loan will be granted.

Syndication (real estate).
Formal group of investors who pool their funds for investments in real property to gain the advantage of: (1) a larger and more diversified property portfolio than they could purchase individually; (2) research and analysis ability of the sponsor(s); (3) professional management; (4) limited liability; and (5) economies of scale in the administrative costs, including legal, accounting, and investment management.

Tax basis—adjusted (property ownership).

The original tax basis of real property is the cost of that property if purchased, or, with certain exceptions, the fair market value of that property if inherited, and the donor's basis if received as a gift. Tax basis is increased by any gift taxes paid by the donor. The adjusted tax basis of real property is increased by the cost of any capital improvements and reduced by the amount of any accumulated depreciation, which is the total of all depreciation deductions taken with respect to that property.

Tax deductible.

Expenses that reduce the amount of taxable income; for example, medical expenses, charitable deductions, and interest paid.

Tax-deferred income.

Cash flow on which no tax is payable, generally because the depreciation deduction is at least as large as the cash flow and debt service.

Tax incentive.

Corporate or venture vehicles that include major tax-deferring or tax-sheltering characteristics.

Tax-loss carry-forward.

In the filing of corporate or individual tax returns, the deduction of the operating losses of prior years' operations from the profits of the current year before calculating tax liability. If losses exceed the profits of the current year and designated prior years, the balance is carried forward for a designated number of years.

Tax-loss pass-through.

In a limited partnership, the tax loss allocated to limited partners, which may be used by them to offset income from other sources.

Tax preference items.

Investors are subject to a federal tax over and above normal income taxes that is equal to the excess of 14 percent of tax preferences over the greater of $10,000 ($5,000 in the case of married taxpayers filing separate returns) or one-half of the regular federal income tax liability (less certain credits). Tax preferences include, among others, drilling costs and the excess of accelerated depreciation over straight-line depreciation on real property. For noncorporate taxpayers, in taxable years ending prior to 1 January 1979, the excluded portion of net capital gains was also a tax preference item subject to this 15 percent "minimum tax." (For corporate taxpayers, the excluded portion of net capital gains remains an item of tax preference subject to the minimum tax.)

Tax Reform Act of 1976 (TRA).
Federal tax legislation signed 4 October 1976 intended to reduce tax loopholes. One of the purposes of the TRA, as it pertains to real estate, was to stem the so-called artificial losses taken on interest and taxes paid during construction projects; on accelerated depreciation; and on prepaid interest and points used to reduce tax liabilities created from other income.

Tax shelter.
The creation of tax losses to offset an individual's taxable income from other sources and thereby reduce his or her current tax liability.

Tax-sheltered investment.
An investment that has an expectation of economic profit, made even more attractive because of the timing of the profit or the way it is taxed, generally having some or all of the following characteristics: capital gains opportunities, high deductions, deferral of income, depletion, accelerated depreciation, and leverage. The flow-through of tax benefits is a material factor regardless of whether the entity is organized as a private program or a public program. Common forms of tax-sheltered investments include: cattle breeding, cattle feeding, equipment leasing, oil and gas, and real estate.

Totten trusts.
Not really trusts, but special banking arrangements in

which the depositor holds the account "in trust for" another and retains sole ownership of the funds for the rest of his, the depositor's, life.

Treasury bill (T-bill).
A short-term U.S. obligation, maturing as soon as 90 days after issue. T-bills do not pay interest, but instead are sold at a discount from their face value.

Treasury bond.
U.S. government bonds issued in $1,000 units with maturity of five years or longer. They are traded on the market like other bonds.

Treasury note.
U.S. government paper, not legally restricted as to interest rates, with maturities from one to five years.

Trust.
A legal entity in which one person or institution holds and manages property for the benefit of another.

Trustee.
The person who holds trust property for the benefit of another.

Uniform Gifts to Minors Act.
A uniform act in force in most states, enabling a gift of specified types of property to a custodian, to be held for a minor until the minor comes of age.

Unsecured loan.
A loan made by a bank based on the borrower's credit history and ability to repay the obligation. The loan is not secured by collateral, but is made on the signature of the borrower; also called a *straight loan*.

Usury.
The practice of lending money or extending credit at a rate of interest that exceeds the legal limit allowed for that type of transaction by the state whose laws govern the legality of the transaction.

Variable-rate mortgage.
A creative financing technique in real estate that

allows the interest charged on the mortgage to fluctuate with the rise and fall of market interest rates.

Will.

A document in which an individual provides for the distribution of property or wealth after death. State law determines distribution if no will is provided. The three types of wills are: (1) *holographic,* which is written entirely by hand and is dated and signed; (2) *formal,* which is a witnessed document; and (3) *noncupative,* which is an oral statement communicated and witnessed at a time of probable death.

Wraparound financing.

A debt instrument that results from the creation of an all-inclusive promissory note (AIPN) or a contract of sale. It leaves intact existing debt on real property (i.e., underlying loan) and may be utilized in the sale or purchase of property. (For example: a seller's building is encumbered by a $70,000 mortgage at 10 percent interest. Seller sells building for $100,000, with $15,000 down, and carries back an $85,000 all-inclusive note at 12 percent interest. From the payments on the $85,000 note, the seller will discharge the payments required on the $70,000 note; therefore, the seller's equity in the all-inclusive note is $15,000.) Wraparound financing usually enables the seller to delay recognition of full capital gains, thereby deferring tax liability, until the wraparound note is paid off.

Yield.

The dividends or interest paid by a company expressed as a percentage of the current price. A stock with a current market value of $20 a share that has paid $1 in dividends in the preceding twelve months is said to return 5 percent ($1.00/$20.00). The current yield on a bond is figured the same way; also known as *return*.

Index

consumer, and interest deductions, 166
discounted sale of, 79
evaluation of, by present value method, 110–11
fixed rate, 8
fully amortizing, and property values, 110
hypothecation, 79, 80–84
nonrecourse, 141–42, 145
on real estate, and banks, 83. *See also* Loans, hypothecation
terms of, 84
Los Angeles County, rent control in, 67

M-1, 7 *chart*, 46
M-1B, 22–23, 168, 169
M-2, 7 *chart*, 46
Management, importance of, 64
Mark, German. *See* Deutschmark
Market, imperfect, 65
Marmon Group, Inc., 28
Mergers (acquisitions), effect of major, on the money supply, 169
and investment opportunities, 27–28
Minneapolis Federal Reserve Bank, 165–66
Missouri Pacific, 28
Mobile home parks, as investments, 156
Monetary Controls Act (1980), 171
Money, fair return on, 110–11
Money market:
changes in, 170–71
demand accounts, 8
instruments of, and the price of gold, 43–44, 45 *chart*, 47
rate accounts, 80
Money supply (M-1, M-1B, M-2) (*see also* Federal Reserve Board and):
components of, 6
economic growth and, 175–77, 176 *chart*
historical trend in, 7 *chart*
increasing, 6–8
and inflation, 165
reporting on, 168–69
Mortgages:
guaranteed, 172
interest rates of, 79
negative amortization of, 72
shared equity, 72
variable-rate, 72
Multifamily housing (*see also* Apartment complexes):
construction financing for, 62
opportunities for investing in, 57–68
outlook for, 154–55
supply and demand for, 60–67, 61

chart
trends of, as an investment, 67–68
Mutual funds:
gold stock, 50
growth, 154

Nabisco, Inc., 28
NASDAQ Index, 151
National debt, the, 165
New York City, rent control in, 67
Nonrecourse financing. *See* Loans, nonrecourse

Occupancy:
levels of, 62
rate, 155. *See also* Vacancy rate
OECD. *See* Organization for Economic Cooperation and Development
Office buildings:
appreciation of, 71
as investments, 155–56
need for, 58
Oil:
and gas, subsidies for, 172
imports of, 26, 27
supply of, and the price of gold, 48–49
Organization for Economic Cooperation and Development (OECD), 173–74

Packaging of hypothecation loans, 82
Partnership, real estate (*see also* Syndication):
financial statements of, 129–34
as a gift to minors, 102
obtaining information about, 129–30
and tax planning, 97–104
Plan, tax-exempt qualified, and tax liability, 87–89, 90, 91–94
Polaroid Corp., 152, 154
Politics, and investment opportunities, 23, 24, 26
Price/earnings ratio, effect of inflation on, 59
Productivity, and interest rates, 17
Property (*see also* Real estate):
business, purchase leaseback of, 156
industrial, as an investment, 156
Pullman Inc., 28

Rate of return:
after tax, 112–24
average, 119, 120
calculating internal, 119–22
RCA Corp., 28

of hypothecation loans, 81–82
legislation about, 62, 64
  and investment in real estate, 29
  and joint ventures, 72–73
  and personal savings, 80
on leveraged investments, 91
reduction in, 161
timing of deductions and, 123–25
Tax Equalization and Fiscal Responsibility
  Act of 1982, 62, 64
Tax Reform Act (1976), 99
Tax shelter, 124
  benefits, 145–46
  internal rate of return and, 146
  and risk, 145–46
Tenneco Chemicals, Inc., 28
Texas Instruments, Inc., 152, 154
Third-world, investment in, 26
3M Co., 152, 154
"Tobin's Q," (a study), 27
Trading up, and taxation, 157
Trans-Union Financial Corp., 28
Treasury, investments of the, 167
Treasury bills:
  calculating risk in, 140
  evaluating, 140
Trusts, irrevocable, and real estate
  partnerships, 97, 99–101

Unemployment rate, and federal
  revenues, 173
Uniform Gifts to Minors Act, 104
  and real estate partnerships, 97,
    101–102
Union Bank, 24
Union Pacific Railroad, 28
Unionism, and housing, 67
United States of America:
  attitude of, toward the gold standard,
    37–38
  foreign investment in, 23–27
  savings rates in, 15
University of Michigan Survey Research
  Center, 12

Vacancy rates, 63 chart
Valuation of a nonliquid real estate limited
  partnership, 100–101
Vietnam, financing war in, 170
Volker, Paul, 6, 64, 47

West Germany, investment in, 26
Wheat futures, calculating risk in, 140–41
Wheelabrator-Fry, Inc., 28
Wilshire Composite Index, 151
World Bank, 38

"X" factor. See Risk, in investments

Yen, 21, 38
Yield, on property sale, 121–24